MEMORIES OF THE PALACE CINEMA

AN ALTON ORAL HISTORY PROJECT

— ABBE FLETCHER —

I0112225

KU
PRESS

ISBN 978-1-909362-81-9

Typeset in: Baskerville, Espiritu, Blakely
Front Cover photo by © Mick Collins. Cover design by Sam Mangan.

Editorial and Design by Kingston University MA Publishing Students: Ally McAlpine, Gemma Haimes, Sam Mangan and Veronica S. Rodriguez Garcia.

KINGSTON UNIVERSITY PRESS
Kingston University
Penrhyn Road
Kingston-upon-Thames
KT1 2EE

This book is dedicated to the people of Alton, Hampshire

and everyone who went to and enjoyed

the Palace Cinema over the years.

The Palace may be closed, but the memories live on.

Notes on the Memories of the Palace Cinema Oral History Project

'Everyone can remember their first cinema experience, a memory which often captures an emotion as much as a particular time in their life. In an age when many social and technological trends seem to be encouraging greater self-reliance and isolation, cinemas above all bring people together to enjoy the shared, communal big screen experience. For many communities, the presence of a local cinema is a source of immense pride.

Often it is the last remaining 'neutral' shared space, accessible to people of all ages and from all backgrounds. As a result, cinemas have taken on an increasingly important social and community as well as cultural role, one supported at many locations by specific screening programmes for older people, for parents and babies and for people with disabilities. The challenges of recent years have unfortunately seen a number of cinemas forced to close. While the individual circumstances can vary, each closure provokes a sense of loss within the local community and the need to reflect on what the venue had offered and the memories it had given to those who have been part of its audience.'

Phil Clapp
Chief Executive, UK Cinema Association

'As a place of dreams, experiences and community, a local cinema is much more than a building! We've been inspired and moved by the Memories of the Palace Cinema Alton Team and their heartfelt oral history work to capture this special history and ensure that watching film together continues to be a part of the life of the town.'

Corinna Downing
Co-owner Palace Cinema, Broadstairs

'Ever since I was a very young child I have had an interest and love for art deco cinemas. Sadly, my own local art deco cinema, the Savoy, Fareham, closed in the 1960s and I set about trying to find out who its architect was, so that I might find similar buildings to visit and enjoy. As part of the process of writing my book I was lucky to be able to closely study the cinemas still operating, including the Palace in Alton, which was one of Mr. Thomas's upgrades in 1937. I had hours of pleasure photographing these buildings and meeting their operators. It is disappointing that, generally speaking, so many cinemas have now gone but, of the three R.A. Thomas cinemas that remain (Ritz, Burnham-on-Sea, three screens, the Plaza, Romsey - now a theatre and the Plaza, Dorchester, four screens), there is fortunately a real determination to preserve and advance well into the future. Long may they, and others, continue to fly the flag!'

Mick Collins
Author of The Cinemas of R. A. Thomas (2015)

The Palace Cinema, © Ally McAlpine

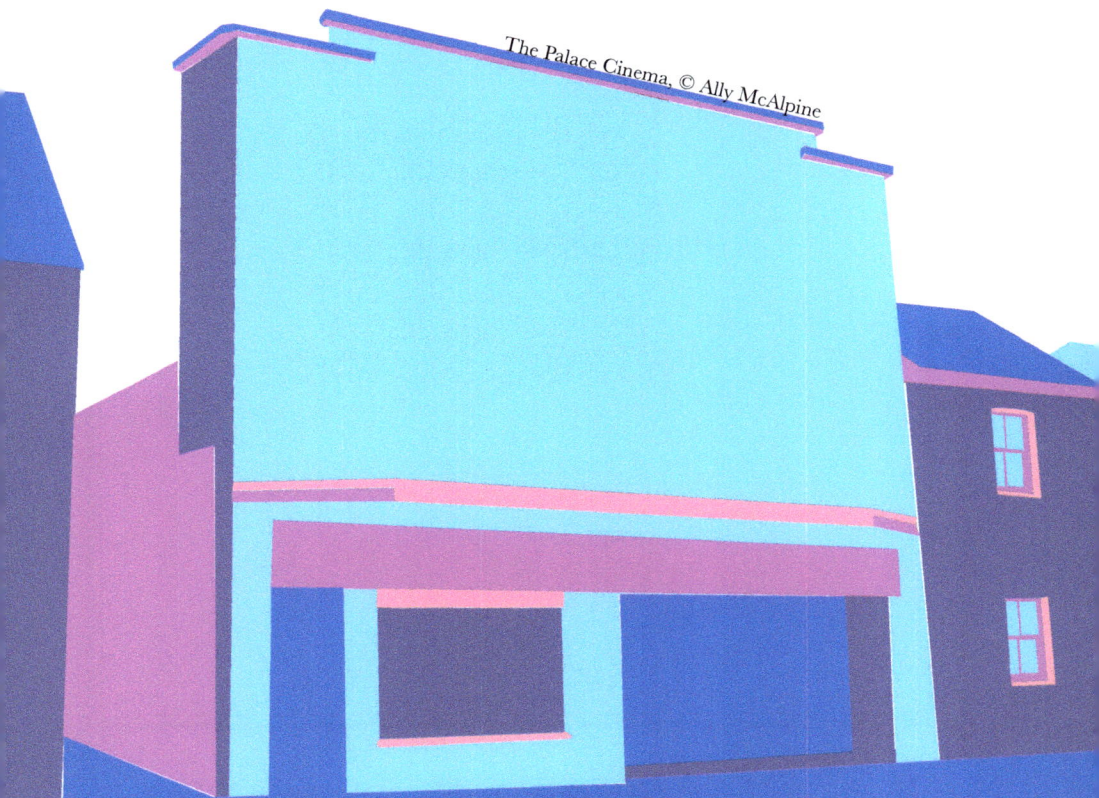

CONTENTS

CONTENTS

CONTENTS

CONTENTS

Notice of opening,1912. ©Hampshire Herald and Alton Gazette. Photo © Mick Collins

Programme from 'Alton's Super Talkie House',1933. Photo © the Curtis Museum Archive

Palace Cinema, Alton, Hampshire. Photo © Phillip Bragg

Foreword

Almost all of Alton's residents, if they have lived here for a few years, will have memories of the Palace Cinema. My own memories date back to the 1970s to the years when there was a weekly disco at the Palace, dancing around our handbags springs to mind and impromptu line ups to dance to the latest Status Quo single in the charts, fun filled times and happy memories.

From school days I remember a visit to watch *Nicholas and Alexandra*, a film about the Russian Royal family, which sparked a life-long interest in history.

Later my own children would regularly attend screenings at the Palace, the local cinema being their first remembered visit to a cinema. In later years the cinema became remembered for its faded grandeur but it is hoped that the exterior will be preserved and I commend the efforts of the Guild of Optimists for drawing together so many memories of the Palace to be remembered for future generations of Altonians.

Cllr Ginny Boxall
Mayor of Alton 2022-23

Cinema is often viewed as the most accessible art form and the most popular with a large proportion of the UK population visiting a cinema at least once a year. Like all great art forms though, it has the ability to change people's lives – to make them feel differently about themselves, to feel connected within their own communities and with those across the world and to give space and time to all the great human emotions, love, grief, hope, despair. Like all art forms, film can change and challenge the way people think about themselves and their place in the world, stimulating ideas, creativity, ambition, and imagination. There is no substitute for watching films together in a communal setting – it is an empowering experience, and often transformational.

This book contains many beautiful memories of the Palace Cinema in Alton, what was, a dearly loved local cinema. The desire to serve a local audience is at the heart of community cinema and at its best can promote cohesion and strong communication within rural and urban communities and boost audiences' film choices; whilst increasing the reach of cinema, particularly in rural areas where there is often otherwise a lack of access. They prioritise what matters most to local audiences, bringing them cinema and stories from beyond the mainstream. They create a sense of place, enriching quality-of-life and transforming local economies.

Over the decades there have been many times when the death knell has tolled for cinema – the advent of new technologies and different modes of viewing have sometimes threatened the fragile ecosystem, particularly of local cinema and its place in the community and sometimes very sadly, we lose them. Cinema however, continues to survive and thrive, it re-invents itself and finds new places. This is because there is no substitute for the magical space where the lights go down and you sit among strangers and experience something new together in that powerful and transformative bright light.

Catharine Des Forges
Director of the Independent Cinema Office

Introduction

Welcome to the Memories of the Palace Cinema

With its large, flat Art Deco frontage, the Palace Cinema makes a striking impression at 58 Normandy St in the market town of Alton, Hampshire, a small, independent cinema with a long history, that has stood in the same spot for more than 110 years since it opened as the Alton Picture Theatre in 1912. It was Alton's first purpose-built cinema, but not the first cinema. Films had been shown in Alton from as early as 1902 in the Assembly Rooms, which was known as the Alton Cinema, and at Alton Electric Theatre at the Forrester's Hall on Church Street from 1911. Plans for the Alton Picture Theatre were agreed in October 1911 and the cinema opened its doors on Wednesday, 18th December 1912.

The Opening Announcement for the Alton Picture Theatre

'Next week Alton will have another picture theatre opened. This latest addition to the town's places of amusement is situated in Normandy Street, opposite the Congregational Church. It has been specially built for the purpose, and the hall is the longest and most commodious in the town, while the directors of the company have spared neither time nor money to fit it out and furnish it in the most up-to-date manner possible. The new building has a striking appearance with a semi-circular front of brick, faced with Bath Stone dressings, and adds an architectural feature to a part of the town which is rather devoid of attractiveness.

Round the arch of the roof the words 'Alton Picture Theatre' are picked out in Bath Stone, raised letters, while underneath in a circular stone the three letters 'A.P.T.' are worked into a monogram. The frontage extends to 40 feet 7 inches, and on one side of the entrance hall accommodation has been found for business premises. The front of the building is finished with solid teak, giving a rich and attractive aspect. The entrance hall is 19 feet wide, and nine steps of terrazzo marble lead to the landing of granitolithic, in front of a highly ornamental pay box, picked out in white. A passage on either side leads to the auditorium, the stage being at the rear end. Once inside the audience will be struck with the size and lofty character of the building.

The area measures 46 feet wide by 62 feet from the back of the hall to the front of the proscenium. In accordance with the plan adopted in all modern theatres and places of amusement the floor is a sloping one, the back seats being on a level with the floor of the stage which is 4 ft high. Those in the back will therefore have an uninterrupted view of the stage which is something new in Alton halls. A feature of the building is the lofty ornamental arched roof which is fitted with patent ventilators sufficient to keep the air of the hall pure and wholesome. The stage measures 27 feet across, and is 17 feet 9 inches deep, and it has been so constructed that an additional 6 feet can if necessary be added in front, making a total depth of nearly 24 feet. Two large dressing rooms are provided, one on either side of the stage. The County Council regulations are rather generous in the way of space for seating regulations for 440 people, leaving a 3 feet gangway down the middle, and a 5 foot vacant space at the rear of the seats. The proscenium is highly ornamental and of a very attractive design.

The usual offices for ladies and gentlemen and a manager's room are provided, with entrances from the passage leading to the hall. The walls are coloured peacock blue, picked out in white and gold, giving the whole place a very dainty and handsome appearance. The operator's room is on the roof over the front entrance, the pictures being projected on to the screen through apertures high up in the back wall behind the audience. Two powerful bioscope arc lanterns have been installed. The hall is most comfortably furnished, the floor being laid with cork lino, and the seats are of most comfortable pattern, and handsome design with shields backs and tip-up seats upholstered in light blue plush. The building will be lit by electricity through out, the power being provided by a horizontal gas engine of 250 r.p.m., which is housed in an engine house built at the rear of the stage. The engine is one supplied by the British Westinghouse Electric Co., of Manchester and London, and drives a 100 amperes 75 *volt compound generator. A switch board in the operating room controls the voltage of the generator, the bioscope arc lanterns, and general lighting of the building. The front is brilliantly illuminated with electric lights. The hall will be heated with gas radiators which work automatically.*

The architect is Mr Bates White, late of Portsmouth and Petersfields, and now of Winnipeg, Canada. Mr Samuel Salter of Southsea is the builder. Messrs E E Taylor, electrical engineers of Cannon Street, are responsible for the electric fittings and the gas radiators are by Messrs Wright & Co of Birmingham. The company which has built the hall has several similar picture theatres in Portsmouth and the South of England, and it will place the very best films obtainable on the programme. There will be two shows each night. It is also intended, we believe to let the hall for theatrical and other entertainments, and with the largest floor space in the town, and one of the largest stages in the South of England, good companies ought to be attracted to the town.'

Hampshire Herald and Alton Gazette
Saturday, 14th December 1912

With the coming of sound, the talkies arrived in Alton in 1931 with *The Desert Song*. The Palace Cinema, as it was now named. It earned itself the nickname 'Alton's Super Talkie House'.

The cinema closed in 1937 for alterations by Robin Audrey Thomas, who designed several Art Deco cinemas in the South of England. Mick Collins author of the 2015 study of Thomas' cinema architecture, along with R. A. Thomas' grandson, established the current façade was part of Thomas' design and part of the major alterations of 1937.

The cinema continued to show films until 1969, when it closed for redecoration and modernisation, reopening with *Thoroughly Modern Millie* in February 1969 as the New Palace Cinema. Bingo began there that same year and continued alongside film screenings until 1984, when the Palace stopped showing films regularly. Wrestling, ballroom dancing, discos and some film screenings continued until the Palace closed again in 1989 for further refurbishment and modernisation.

Normandy Street, ALTON, HANTS. Tel. 103

THE PALACE.

Continuous from 6 p.m. Matinees Wednesday & Saturday at 2.30.

Friday & Saturday, March 6th & 7th—THE LAST OF THE SILENT FILMS—
JACK HOLT and **DOROTHY REVIER** in " **THE TIGRESS** " and **JACQUELINE LOGAN** in " **GIRL OF THE NIGHT.**"

MONDAY, March 9th—

TALKIES ! TALKIES ! ! TALKIES ! ! !

GRAND OPENING ATTRACTION !

JOHN BOLES and **CARLOTTA KING** in

THE DESERT SONG

Supported by **LOUISE FAZENDA, MYRNA LOY, JOHNNY ARTHUR** and **Chorus of Hundreds !**

A staggering succession of bewitching songs presented with boundless magnificence that reaches the unsurmountable heights of unparalleled entertainment—an epochal production that will live for ever in your memory ! !

THURSDAY, March 12th—

A BRITISH TALKIE TO TALK ABOUT !

See and Hear TOM WALLS, RALPH LYNN, MARY BROUGH and **WINIFRED SHOTTER** in

ROOKERY NOOK

A riot of non-stop nonsense ! An all-British Cast in an all-British Comedy ! ! English humour at its best !

GRAND SUPPORTING PROGRAMME OF TALKIE AND SILENT ITEMS !

NOTE.—Owing to the enormous cost of the installation of Talkies, etc., please note slight alteration in prices of admission :—

6d.   9d.   1/2   and   1/6

SPECIAL · MATINEE EACH WEDNESDAY at 2.30.

Seats at 1/6 may be booked at Cinema or at Messrs. Teague & King, High St., Alton

Cars may be parked in Victoria Road, one minute from Cinema !

'The talkies come to the Palace', March 1931. Hampshire Herald and Alton Gazette.
Photo by © Mick Collins

It opened again on Boxing Day 1989 with *The Delinquents* featuring Kylie Minogue.

Raj Jeyasingam took over the cinema in 1994 and put in a second screen with sixty seats in 2003. The Bingo hall was converted into flats in 2014 and the Palace continued to show films seven days a week across its two screens. Like cinemas everywhere, the Palace closed its doors during the pandemic lockdowns of 2020–21 but re-opened afterwards. In December 2021, it was announced that the cinema was up for sale. A campaign was started to try and save the cinema, which is where this project originated, but sadly, it could not be saved.

The Palace Cinema finally closed its doors on Sunday, 30th October 2022. It was talking to people in the Public Gardens in the summer of 2022, while campaigning to keep the Palace Cinema open, that the idea for this project took hold. The people we spoke to spontaneously shared their memories of going to the Palace. For some, this was their first trip to the cinema as children; for others, it was a visit with friends or school. Some people met or went on dates with their partners at the Palace, and it is where they took their children for their first cinema experience. Some still went weekly to see whatever was on – the Palace always had the latest releases to choose from.

While it proved difficult to save the cinema, the idea for an oral history project emerged to record peoples' memories of cinema-going in Alton and to document the fact that our town had a cinema – one of the oldest purpose-built cinemas in the country – for posterity and to keep this archive at the Curtis Museum, which had helped spark the idea for the project with their Memories of Alton Oral History Project.

We launched the Memories of the Palace Cinema Oral History Project on the 24th September 2022 at Alton Community Centre with an event where people could come along and record their memories, some of which were broadcast on the radio. People could contribute to the project by filling out our questionnaire online, or from the Curtis Museum and through interviews with our small research team. We have gathered questionnaire responses and interviews into this book, which we hope you will enjoy perusing. While we held Record Your Memories events at the Community Centre and the Allen Gallery in 2022–23 and had a stand in the Curtis Museum with questionnaires, recording memories was not an exhaustive process; there are, of course, many more memories than we could ever record.

This is just the tip of the iceberg, a collection from the people who responded to our call – there will be many more memories that didn't reach us. But this collection is a salute to the impact that cinema – the films but also the act of watching films together on the big screen and the building itself – can have on generations.

It is a celebration of the Palace Cinema in Alton. This study is only one of many currently happening around the country, as audiences react to the closure of cinemas and cultural art venues feel the cuts to arts and culture funding nationwide. One of our respondents said that she hadn't thought about going to the cinema for a long time and that, in talking to us, she had been given those memories back.

We hope that by reading this book, you will revisit your memories of cinema-going and seek out opportunities to watch films together on the big screen.

Abbe Fletcher
Project Lead Memories of the Palace Cinema
Alton Oral History Project Alton, January 2024

Palace board announcing closure during pandemic, 2020-21.
Photo © Abbe Fletcher

The PALACE

Has been entirely re-built complete with BALCONY.

Tastefully Decorated Throughout in Soft Shades of Pink and Gold with Green as contrast.

Fitted Carpets in the whole of the Auditorium and Balcony with Comfortable Seating.

New Ventilation and Heating Systems have been Installed.

The New Screen Curtain will have several Novel Lighting Effects. The Especially Designed Electrical Fittings are very unusual.

The Exterior has been modernised with Striking Neon Sign and Lighting.

The Prices of Admission have not been altered. They are :—

Stalls : 6d., 9d. and 1/3 (including tax)

Balcony : 1/6 (including tax)

Children at reduced prices except Saturday nights & Bank Holidays.

Future Film Presentations include :—

"O. H. M. S.," the film made with the co-operation of the Army.

"My Man Godfrey," with William Powell and Carole Lombard.

"Windbag The Sailor" and "Good Morning, Boys," both starring Will Hay.

"Song of Freedom," with Paul Robeson.

"Dimples," starring Shirley Temple, etc.

Hampshire Heralds and Alton Gazette Announce Grand Re-opening of the Palace, 1937. Photo by © Mick Collins.

THE PALACE, ALTON

On and from

MONDAY, FEBRUARY 8th

THE PALACE WILL BE

CLOSED FOR RE-BUILDING

▲ A Balcony is to be built together with Lounge

▲ A new Ventilating and Heating System Installed

▲ The Cinema will be Carpeted throughout

▲ The Interior will be Decorated in a Modern and Tasteful Fashion

▲ The Exterior will again be Modernized and Illuminated by Neon Lighting

▲ Novel Lighting Effects will be used on the New Proscenium and Curtain

▲ The New Electrical Fittings are being especially designed

WATCH FOR FURTHER ANNOUNCEMENTS IN

"THE HAMPSHIRE HERALD"

Hampshire Herald and Alton Gazette 'Closed for Re-building',1937. Photo by © Mick Collins

The grand re-opening of the Palace, June 1937. © Hampshire Herald and Alton Gazette.
Photo © Mick Collins

The Alton Picture Theatre, 58 Normandy Street in 1913 (note the lettering in Bath Stone and the central monogram APT described in the opening announcement on page 2). Photo courtesy of Tim Waters

★★★★★ PALACE
★ NEW ★ CINEMA
ALTON 2303

GRAND OPENING SATURDAY
1st MARCH
with

JULIE ANDREWS
MARY TYLER MOORE
CAROL CHANNING
JAMES FOX

ROSS HUNTER'S
"THOROUGHLY
MODERN
MILLIE"

JOHN GAVIN
BEATRICE LILLIE

TIMES:—SAT. SUN. MON. TUES. WED. THUR. FRI. 4.35 p.m. 7.31 p.m.
SUN. 3rd March 3.30 p.m. 7.00 p.m.
SAT. 8th March 1.25 p.m. 4.31 p.m.

Plus
PATHE NEWS

Plus
LOOK AT LIFE

CHILDREN'S CLUB
Every Saturday Morning
10-30
(Doors open 10 a.m.)
First Club Morning Saturday,
8th March

NO INCREASE IN PRICE
Stalls 3/- 4/-
Circle 5/-
Children Half-Price except Saturdays
and Bank Holidays.

Hampshire Herald and Alton Gazette 'Grand Opening' Announcement, 1969.
Photo © Mick Collins.

PALACE CINEMA
ALTON
Tel. (0420) 82303

★ NEW LUXURY STUDIO ★
Opens This Boxing Day
Tuesday, 26th December

FOR 10 DAYS
THE DELINQUENTS (12)
KYLIE MINOGUE and CHARLIE SCHLATTER
Performances every day at 3.20, 6.00 and 8.30 p.m.
(except Sunday, 31st December, 3.20 p.m. ONLY)

THIS IS NOW A NON-SMOKING CINEMA

Future presentations:
INDIANA JONES AND THE LAST CRUSADE
BACK TO THE FUTURE Part II.
GHOSTBUSTERS II.
OLIVER AND COMPANY

Admission prices: Adult £3; Child £1.75
O.A.P. £1.75 before 6.30 p.m.
Advance bookings available by Visa and Access
on evening performances only

The Palace Cinema 'Studio Cinema', Alton, Hampshire, 1989. Photo © Mick Collins

WHAT ARE YOUR THOUGHTS ON THE CLOSING OF THE PALACE CINEMA ON THE 30TH OCTOBER 2022?

Such a shame, it was there for almost 100 years.

Very sad [...] Alton needs a cinema.

VERY SAD INDEED

TRAGIC TO SEE IT GO [...] DESPITE KAT, ABBE AND ANNIE'S BEST EFFORTS. POP UP SOON PLEASE.

A shame as it was always nice to have a local cinema and it's a good wet weather option in the school holidays. VERY VERY SAD AND DISAPPOINTED.

I THINK WE SHOULD TURN THE CINEMA INTO A OLD FASHIONED CINEMA THAT PLAYS OLD CLASSICS. I'VE LOOKED AROUND FOR UNIQUE CINEMA EXPERIENCES AND THERE ISN'T MUCH NEAR ALTON.

A GREAT LOSS OF A HISTORIC ASSET WITH GREAT POTENTIAL.

I am deeply saddened by it but understand why Raj had to sell. I will miss the cinema so much as it is my fave place in Alton. I love the history of it .

DOES ALTON NEED A CINEMA?

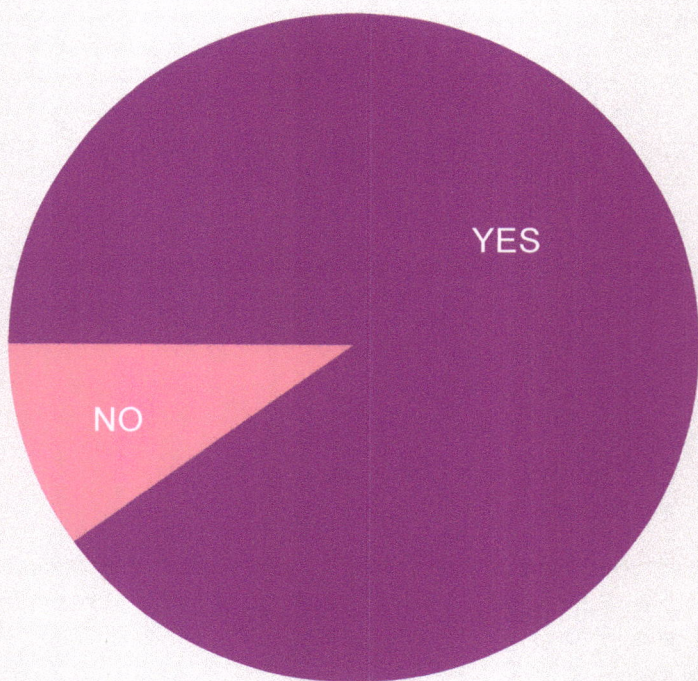

HOW OLD ARE YOU?

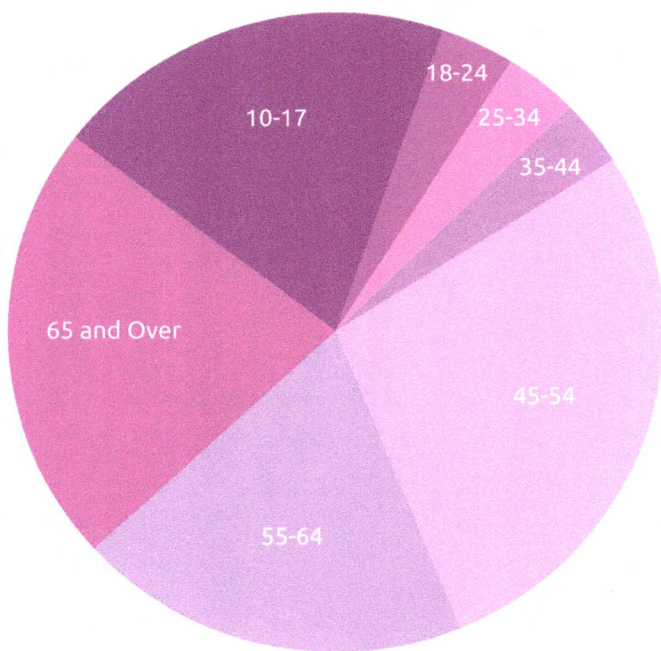

- 18-24
- 25-34
- 35-44
- 10-17
- 45-54
- 65 and Over
- 55-64

THE
PALACE
ALTON.
Phone : 2303.

Christmas Day December 25th, for One Day Only.

CLOSED

Boxing Day, December 26th, for three Days

ALASTAIR SIM, JOYCE GRENFELL,
GEORGE COLE in

THE BELLES
OF ST. TRINIANS

Approx. times of Showing 2.55 p.m., 5.45 p.m. and 8.35 p.m.

U

Also Patrick Bexhill, William Patrick in

The Clue of the Missing Ape

Approx. Times of Showing 1.50 p.m., 4.40 p.m. and 7.30 p.m.

U

Last Complete Programme will Commence at 7.30 p.m.

Times of showing are subject to alteration.

CHILDREN ADMITTED UNACCOMPANIED BY AN ADULT TO THIS PROGRAMME

Palace Cinema Poster, 1954, from Holybourne Rare Books with thanks to Raj Jeyasingam

Raj Jeyasingam
Owner and Manager of the Palace Cinema
1994–2022

I came to Alton to buy the Palace Bingo Club in 1994 and discovered the purchase of the building also included a single-screen cinema. At that time, I had no previous experience in operating a cinema as a business. The previous owner, Mark Eaton, said he would help me for the first three months.

I was lucky to inherit an excellent team of staff, which made my learning experience quite enjoyable. I quickly realised that the cinema on its own could not carry on. The profit from the Bingo Club had to subsidise the cinema business to co-exist.

When a new bingo club opened in Basingstoke, it was very difficult to compete with them as they were paying massive amounts of cash prizes. It was at this time the smoking ban in public places came into effect, causing customers not to visit as many times per week as they used to. Consequently, the bingo business began to suffer. I decided to utilise some of the unwanted space and built a second cinema screen in 2002. I have fond memories of opening the second screen with the film *Chicago*, starring Catherine Zeta-Jones and Renée Zellweger. While I was excited about the birth of the second screen, I was also sad to see the decline of the bingo business, which has subsequently been closed. Many of my bingo customers had become good friends, but sadly, most were in their 80's and 90's and were not able to visit the bingo as much, even though I drove some to and from the hall.

As in independent cinema, we were able to show films for charity fundraising, birthday parties, etc. Because of the responsible and reliable team who were part of the operation, local people used to bring children as young as eight years old and leave them to watch the films on their own. The parents knew that we would do a regular check during the films to ensure no harm would come to their children. Something like this can only happen in an independent cinema.

We used to have groups of friends using the cinema as a regular meeting place, particularly the ladies getting together once a week to see a film and then move on to a restaurant for a meal.

There were times when we used to do special shows for wheelchair users and children with special needs. For example, we used to invite children with sensitive hearing to special shows where we could adjust the volume levels to suit the audience.

Knowing our customers undoubtedly helped me to choose the right films the customers I was catering for enjoyed. We were able to show all the films on their release date as we were able to guarantee that the films would be shown seven days a week. Many other small cinemas would have to wait four weeks after initial release to show new films as they would only show them three days a week. I found that the most popular films in the area would be comedies and dramas – thrillers and horrors were not popular. Some of the most popular sell-out films over the years have included *The Bridges of Madison County*, *Mamma Mia* and the first Harry Potter film. Luckily, after I had upgraded the screens to digital projectors, I was able to show the popular films on both screens simultaneously, which meant no one was turned away.

With the growing reliability of the internet, I decided to start showing live events streamed from the West End. I had a core group of customers who attended these, showing up regularly as it was not always practical for people to travel to London via train and get the last train back. The theatre companies realised that they could put their shows on streaming services for customers to watch at home.

I enjoyed running the cinema in Alton, as I enjoyed seeing children grow up and then bring their own families in to see the films. I have made lots of friends here; unsurprisingly, I probably know more about Alton than I do about my neighbours at home.

Unfortunately, the developing technology has had a detrimental effect on the cinema business: the effects of Netflix, Amazon Prime, etc. And not to mention the rising cost of utilities. These things are beyond our control and have made the business untenable.

Closing the Palace has been one of the hardest decisions I have made; it was my life for 28 years, and although I put it off for nearly five years, in the end, I had to admit defeat and accept the reality that the cinema I own is unlikely to make money in its current configuration. The building, although large, does not make the best use of its space due to the configuration – and ultimately, refurbishing it to modern standards would never recoup the investment required. I admire the other small cinemas out there for hanging on, I know it's not easy for them.

The Palace Cinema, Alton, Hampshire, 2011. Photo © Mick Collins

WHEN DID YOU FIRST VISIT THE PALACE CINEMA IN ALTON?

1972

'I think it would have been 1972 or 3. We came with our school, Eggar's Grammar School, to see Macbeth, which we were studying in English lessons.'

Mid 1970s

'Not certain of exact year or film but probably around mid 1970s to see Disney film - or possibly to see something with the family.'

Early 80s

'Saw Kramer Vs Kramer'

Feb. 2014

'Moved here in late 2013'

1954

1960s

1975

1977

1979

1984

1990s

1991

1992

1996

2008

2009

2013

2016

2017

Around 1978

Probably in about 1978

In the 1950s

During the late 80s

Sometime in 1988-89

It would have been around 2006

2016 (I was 5-6)

About 60 years ago

It wasn't my first time but it was 2020
a few months ago

I don't remember, many years ago
young maybe 4 or 5

Aged 12

HOW FREQUENTLY HAVE YOU VISITED THE PALACE CINEMA, ALTON?

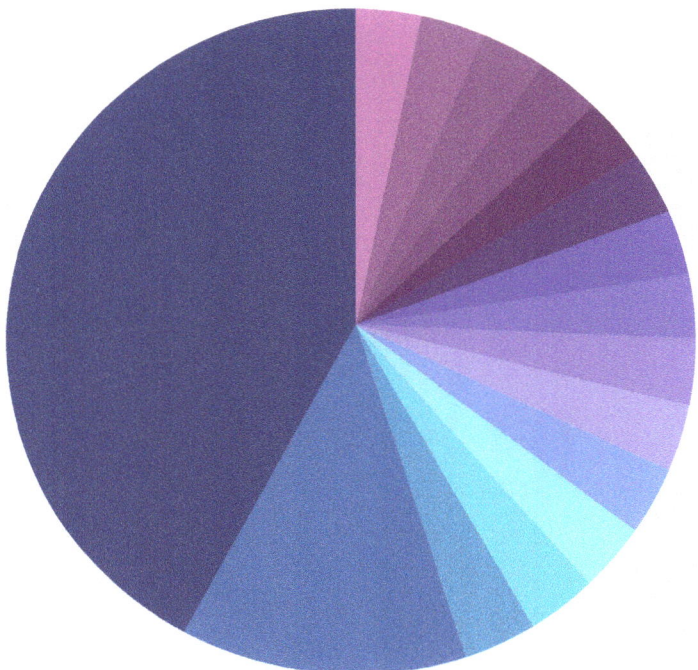

- Frequently
- Under five times
- Yearly
- Monthly
- Weekly
- Never been inside
- Frequently from 1991 until 2008
- Three to four times a year
- Six to ten
- Whenever there was a film on I wanted to see
- Used to go regularly
- A few times as a child
- Four times a year
- Six to twelve times a year
- Every half term
- Weekly as a child

Memories of the Palace Cinema in Alton, Hampshire, Launch Event, 2022.
Photo © Abbe Fletcher

Kat Guenioui being interviewed by Chris Stone at the Memories of the Palace Cinema Launch event in Alton, Hampshire, 2022.
Photo © Abbe Fletcher

Abbe Fletcher & Kat Geunoui
Interview by Chris Stone
Memories of the Palace Cinema Launch
24th September 2022

Chris Stone: Talking to Abbe Fletcher, who has set up projects for capturing memories of the Palace Cinema. I was wondering if you'd like to tell us a little bit more about the project?

Abbe Fletcher: Yes. We've been talking to people around the town about the Palace Cinema and just noticing how people seem to share their memories with us while we're talking about it. This seemed like something we should record, for posterity: the fact that there's a cinema in Alton and it's been around for a very long time, and that people have used that cinema and enjoyed it over generations. The memories that we're hearing were just really quite fantastic, about growing up with a cinema in the town. So to capture that and to document the cinema, that was really the inspiration for the project. Then the idea is to build an archive of those memories and to give it to the Curtis Museum to contribute to their local history collection and to document the fact that there is and has been a cinema in Alton since 1912.

C.S. Am I right in thinking that you have a little bit of background in film knowledge?

A.F. Yes. I teach at Kingston University. I am a course leader for a Masters in Filmmaking there. I'm a bit of a cinephile if you will, so all things film. The cinema is really part of why we moved to Alton. Seeing this independent cinema in this market town was a big draw for us. Cinema and films are very big in our household.

C.S. Moving things forward, I've got Kat Guenioui with me here, who is part of a group of people who are looking into the possibility of continuing the cinema possibilities in Alton. Is that right?

Kat Guenioui: Yes. That's the reason that we started our investigations into saving the cinema. We've always felt that the town could support a cinema. There's nothing about Alton that makes it so that a cinema can't work in the town. When the Palace closes, we'll continue our work, hoping to find another way to bring cinema to the people of Alton. Whether that's a pop-up cinema or a community cinema, that's what we would love. We would love to say that, though the Palace may close, cinema will continue in Alton. The Palace wasn't the first cinema in Alton, so it doesn't need to be the last.

C.S. I just assumed that the Palace Cinema was the only cinema that Alton has had, but apparently, there were two?

A.F. Yes. There was a cinema in Alton in 1911 at the Forrester's Hall on Church Street, and before that, films were shown at the Assembly Rooms. The Palace was the first purpose-built cinema in Alton, but it's fantastic to think of Alton being a hub of cinemas that early on. It's surprising.

C.S. Something special about Alton itself to have a purpose-built cinema. Kat, have you got any particular memories of films that you've been to see?

K.G. I remember going to see a Bond film at the Palace Cinema. I can't remember which one it was, but that was quite an experience. There were lots of people there and it was just really well-received. I know that people will say you can watch a film at home, but I think going to the cinema and watching a film with other people where you're laughing together, crying together, it's a shared experience. You come out feeling closer to the people around you. I think Alton has got a wonderful community, and we would benefit from sharing more experiences together, like the cinema. Even the Car Show, [one of the] the many things that the town offers, so why not have a nice cinema that we can all attend together?

C.S. Thank you both for taking the time to talk to us, thank you.

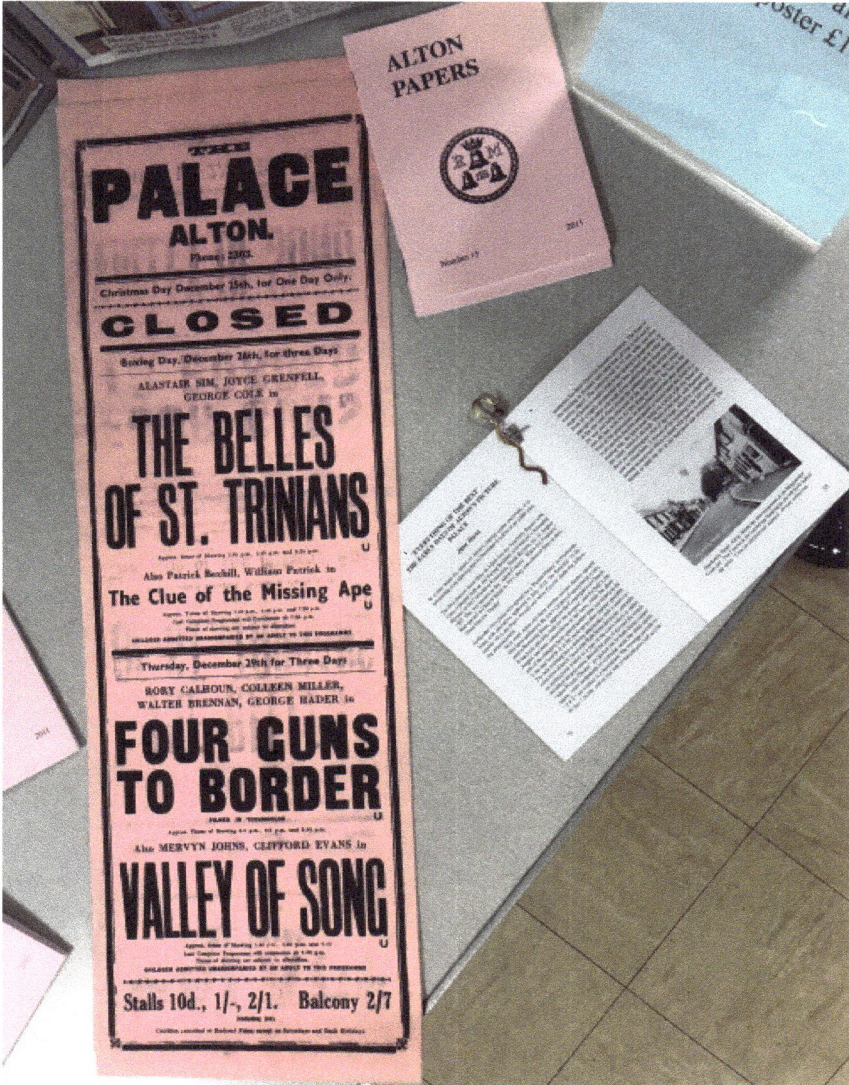

Memories of the Palace Cinema in Alton, Hampshire, Launch Event, 2022.
Photo © Abbe Fletcher

HOW DO YOU TRAVEL TO THE PALACE CINEMA, ALTON?

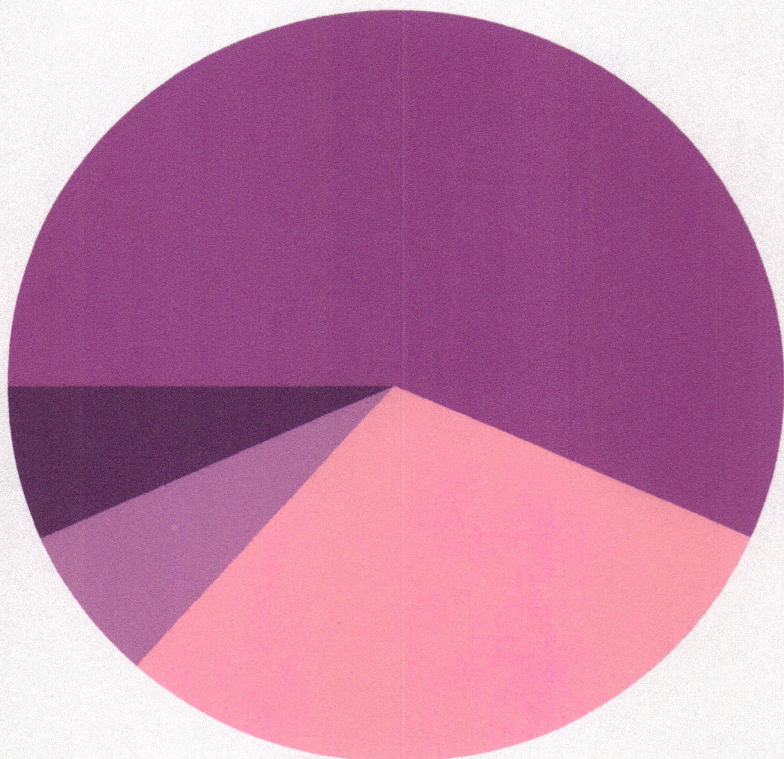

- Walk
- Drive
- Public transport
- Don't visit now

WHAT REFRESHMENTS WOULD YOU BUY OR TAKE THERE?

Ice creams
Always popcorn!
Homemade popcorn
a bottle of coke!
Fanta
Revels
Drinks
Beer as teenagers
Kia Ora orange
Crisps
Sweets
Fanta
Mars bars
Popcorn
A box of fruit pastilles
Cheesy biscuits
Can't remember
I'd sneak sweets in
Generally wouldn't buy or take anything
Orange drink had to pop a straw in the top

WHAT DO YOU REMEMBER ABOUT YOUR FIRST VISIT?

Enjoying the film and good company.

Went with my dad and I loved the atmosphere. Its not daunting like Vue or Odeon cinema which are so big.

The size of the screen and the decor.

It was my daughters first ever time in a cinema as she was only three.

DELIGHTED!   Taking my young nieces and nephew.

The dark velvet seats and being given a jamboree bag of sweets when coming out.

Balcony, usherette, two films.

Went to see *Star Wars* on a Tuesday afternoon, when I should have been at school.

My grandad took us I think it was *Snow White* and we sat in the balcony.

I liked how near it was and that it was a cozy little cinema.

I was really excited, jumping up and down and whispering to my mother and friend until we got shushed. It was *The Secret Life of Pets*, and we got toffee popcorn from Raj. In the end, after all that excitement, halfway through I was scared witless by the bunny who broke out of the pet pound.

Nice and local.

IT WAS SATURDAY MORNING KIDS CLUB; THE FILMS WERE IN COLOUR AND WE GOT A BAG OF SWEETS. IT WAS AMAZING.

I think there was just a single screen – one film per week. Well attended. Queuing outside – sometimes having to sit too near to the front!

My friend from sixth form was a part time projectionist there. We used to go sometimes when he was working.

This was my 3 year old daughters first trip to a cinema. She was very excited and insisted on sitting in the middle of the front row. Just as the lights dimmed I was delighted to see six or eight young children (from Raj's family) file in and sit cross-legged in front of us.

Nostalgic. Just very homely.

It was really good. Everyone could see because it was just me and my mate in there. We sat at the front eating sweets.

I remember seeing *Jurassic Park* at the Palace Cinema, Alton. I was with friends in the front row and it felt like the dinosaurs were coming out of the screen at me, it was exciting and exhilarating. I remember feeling younger, though working it out, I must have been 17. A neighbour had taken a group of us and it was a fun trip, with muffled shrieks and giggles – having a great time. The screen felt huge and it was a vivid experience.

I REMEMBER IT WAS VERY BIG, IT WAS EXCITING, I LOVED GOING THERE. WE WOULD SIT DOWNSTAIRS AND IN THE BALCONY.

PALACE CINEMA
Tel. ALTON 82303

TOMORROW, WED. (6th April):
ROBERT REDFORD — DUSTIN HOFFMAN
ALL THE PRESIDENT'S MEN (AA)
5.00 & 7.57

Also: CARTOONS
7.25

THURSDAY, 7th April:
WRESTLING
See separate advertisement

SUNDAY, 10th April — 7 days:
Note times below
WALT DISNEY'S ever popular
BAMBI (U)
Sunday 5.06 & 8.12
Monday, Wednesday & Thursday 2.00 5.06 8.12
Tuesday, Friday & Saturday 2.00 only

Also
THE STRONGEST MAN IN THE WORLD (U)
Sunday 6.23
Monday, Wednesday & Thursday 3.17 & 6.23
Tuesday, Friday & Saturday 3.17 only

PLEASE NOTE — THERE ARE NO EVENING FILM
SHOWINGS ON TUESDAYS, FRIDAYS OR SATURDAYS

Palace Cinema adverts in the Hampshire Herald and Alton Gazette: Ten Commandments (1960), Bonnie and Clyde (1968), All the Presidents Men & Bambi (1977).
Photo © Abbe Fletcher

THE PALACE
ALTON'S LUXURY CINEMA
Telephone Alton 2303   Free Public Car Park Opp. Cinema

THURSDAY, 14th MARCH — FOR THREE DAYS
That 3 Million Pound Train Robbery !
Stanley Baker   Joanna Pettet   James Booth
ROBBERY (U)
Eastman Colour   2.49   5.32   8.15

Walt Disney's
A COUNTRY COYOTE GOES TO HOLLYWOOD (U)
Technicolor   2.00   4.43   7.26

SUNDAY, 17th MARCH — FOR ONE DAY ONLY
Stewart Granger   Raf Vallone   Mickey Rooney   Henry Silva
THE SECRET INVASION (A)
Colour   5.00   8.40

Henry Silva   Elizabeth Montgomery   Sammy Davis, Jr.
JOHNNY COOL (A)
6.47

MONDAY, 18th MARCH—FOR SIX DAYS   The Year's Most Sensational Film!

WARREN BEATTY
FAYE DUNAWAY

THEY'RE YOUNG...
THEY'RE IN LOVE...
AND THEY
KILL PEOPLE

BONNIE AND CLYDE
MICHAEL J. POLLARD · GENE HACKMAN · ESTELLE PARSONS, DAVID NEWMAN and ROBERT BENTON
Produced by WARREN BEATTY ARTHUR PENN TECHNICOLOR A WARNER BROS.—SEVEN ARTS RELEASE

Mon.-Fri.   2.54   5.39   8.24   Sat.   5.40   8.25
COMPANY OF FOOLS (U)
Technicolor   2.00   4.45   7.30   Sat.   4.45   7.30

SATURDAY, 23rd MARCH — At 2.00 Only   Special All-U Matinee
Gordon Scott in SAMSON AND THE 7 MIRACLES (U) Technicolor
Jeffrey Hunter in MAN FROM GALVESTON (U) Technicolor

THE PALACE
ALTON'S LUXURY CINEMA
Tel. ALTON 2303

THURSDAY, NOVEMBER 3, for Three Days
DORIS DAY   DAVID NIVEN
PLEASE DON'T EAT THE DAISIES (U)
Delightful—Delirious—Delicious
(CinemaScope   Colour)   2.0, 5.10, 8.20
Also LAUREL AND HARDY   NOTHING BUT TROUBLE (U)
3.50, 7.0
Children admitted unaccompanied   Last performance will commence at 7 p.m.

SUNDAY, NOVEMBER 6   Doors Open 4.45 p.m.   Commence 5 p.m.
Richard Basehart, Phyllis Kirk CANYON CROSSROADS (U)
John Bromfield, Julie London   CRIME AGAINST JOE (A)

MAGNIFICENT UNPRECEDENTED SPECTACLE
MONDAY, NOV. 7th, for SIX Days
Two Separate Performances
Doors open 1.45 and 6 p.m.
Showing approx. at 2.10 and 6.25 p.m.

Cecil B De Mille's production
THE TEN (U)
COMMANDMENTS

CHARLTON   YUL   ANNE   EDWARD G.
HESTON   BRYNNER   BAXTER   ROBINSON
Yvonne DE CARLO   Debra Paget   John DEREK
SIR CEDRIC   NINA   MARTHA   JUDITH   VINCENT
HARDWICKE   FOCH   SCOTT   ANDERSON   PRICE

TECHNICOLOR   VISTAVISION

Prices of Admission:
Balcony 5/-; Children 2/6
Stalls 3/6, 2/6; Children 2/-, 1/6
Old Age Pensioners 1/6
Special Rates for Parties of 30 and over
School Children, Religious Groups, etc.,
apply the Manager

Bob Booker & Jo Holmes

Interview by Chris Stone
Memories of the Palace Cinema Launch
24th September 2022

Chris Stone: Very lucky to be talking to Jo Holmes and Bob Booker, with us here to share your memories of the Palace Cinema. If I could come to you first, Jo, are there any particular films that you remember seeing back in the day?

Jo Holmes: Yes. Probably the biggest one as a child was *Snow White and the Seven Dwarfs* on a massive screen in colour. We children were there on a Saturday morning, there must have been a couple of hundred and it was absolutely quiet, you could have dropped a pin. The kids, their eyes were out on stalks, just watching this wonderful film.

C.S. I bet it must've been something to watch on the big screen.

J.H. It was awesome. It was sad and funny, the children would laugh, then get quiet. Yes. Brilliant. I used to attend the morning ones. That was where most of the children used to go.

C.S. You went as well, Bob?

Bob Booker: I went in the afternoon with my sisters. I can recall that very well because the children themselves, and I'm sure Jo will recollect this as well, were pretty raucous to begin with. There was a lot of noise and everyone looking at their mates who were up in the gallery or in the stalls around the corner. As soon as the features started, silence descended, then you had the laughter and the tears or the various features. Certainly, when I went in the afternoon, there were always two features. One was the cartoon, which if you remember, Jo, it was *Tom and Jerry*-

J.H. Yes, brilliant.

31

B.B. -and some of the others. They were always brilliant.

J.H. *Bugs Bunny.*

'WE CHILDREN WERE THERE ON A SATURDAY MORNING, THERE MUST HAVE BEEN A COUPLE OF HUNDRED AND IT WAS ABSOLUTELY QUIET, YOU COULD HAVE DROPPED A PIN.'

B.B. Everyone was cheering when they'd come on, so it'd be about five, ten minutes, then they'd have the main feature. The one I recall that really stuck in my memory was *The Vikings* with Tony Curtis and Kirk Douglas. We were playing *The Vikings* for many, many days after that.

C.S. Obviously, going to the cinema, you don't necessarily go and just watch the film. You have some sort of refreshments. Jo, I think you were saying there was a sweet shop next door.

J.H. Yes. There was a sweet shop next door. I think there were sweets inside in the little kiosk. I think most of the kids would get them outside and then take them in with them.

C.S. Ice creams as well?

J.H. Oh, yes. There was a lady, who used to come around with a little tray of tubs and lollies and things.

C.S. Humorous stories, I'm sure neither of you did that, but what did some people do with their leftover ice cream cones?

J.H. Oh, yes. The people in the gods (balcony) would often throw their ice cream tubs over and onto us sitting down below.

C.S. Did they just turn up and watch the film?

J.H. We'd all queue up and go in and sit down and you'd find your mates and go and sit with them.

C.S. No adults or parents with them?

B.B. Kind of, my recollection, Jo, and you may recall as well, was that the lady who did the ice creams also did the tickets and she kind of kept an eye on us.

J.H. Yes.

B.B. If anyone was causing a little bit too much trouble then they were dealt with. I don't recall anyone being grabbed by the scruff of the neck and taken out. I certainly do recall the fact that when the feature started, things did calm down. It was packed. I have a memory of them always being full. Some of the people would bring their sweets in, of course, because they were a little bit cheaper than they were in the cinema. We always had money for the ice cream. My favourite was the choc-ice. We always had choc-ices. Of course, you'd come out with chocolate all around your mouth and everyone knew where you'd been.

> ## 'WE DIDN'T GET TELEVISION TILL THE LATE '50S, AND YOU'D GO TO THE CINEMA TO SEE THE PATHÉ NEWS, WHICH GAVE YOU THE WORLDWIDE NEWS.'

C.S. I think, Jo, you were saying about the Pathé News?

J.H. In those days, you had your paper. This was before television. We didn't get television till the late 1950s, and you'd go to the cinema to see the Pathé News, which gave you the worldwide news. It was always in black and white, but it was always something, especially the football, you used to get the little football bits from the first division. Of course, all your superstars were up there and you'd watch them there.

C.S. Have either of you got a particular little anecdote or a humorous story that you can remember from the cinema?

J.H. I was saying earlier that if we'd run out of pocket money, one of our friends would go in and walk past the fire exit and just touch it with his bottom, it would just open, and the rest of us would come in that way. My brother said he was in the back of the stalls, they had heavy red, velvet curtains. As we went through one at a time, he said, these curtains kept going like somebody was sending Morse code.

C.S. Brilliant.

J.H. It was all of us. There was a character, do you remember? I think he was at the chief usherette. It was his job to come in with his torch. He used to go in like a big searchlight. He used to say, 'Quiet children'. You'd get a rude answer back. He'd said, 'Who said that? Who said that?'

B.B. I'm one of those guys that was always interested in girls, even at that age, eight or nine. I remember making arrangements to meet a girlfriend in the cinema. Of course, in those days you try and get to the back because you're not disturbed then, by other people who are watching the feature film. I remember being really worried because I knew she had another boyfriend and I just wanted to have a real good look around and check that he wasn't there because then there would be trouble. It was always a place to meet in secret.

C.S. Absolutely fascinating talking to you both. Many, many thanks.

J.H. You're welcome.

'IT WAS ALWAYS A PLACE TO MEET IN SECRET.'

The Palace Cinema in Alton, Hampshire, 2011.
Photo © Mick Collins

The Palace Cinema in Alton, Hampshire, 2024.
Photo © Abbe Fletcher

WHAT DO YOU REMEMBER ABOUT THE PALACE CINEMA AT THAT TIME?

IT WAS AN ATTRACTION IN OUR CHOICE OF TOWN TO RE-LOCATE TO. TWO SCREENS WITHIN EASY WALKING DISTANCE.

THERE WAS ONE SCREEN AND YOU COULD SIT ON THE UPPER BALCONY LEVEL.

THE ADVERTS! THE TRAILERS.

QUIRKY, UNIQUE VENUE.

IT WAS BEAUTIFUL. SO BIG INSIDE.

I got popcorn and the screen was so big and it was the first time going to a cinema.

It was quiet and intimate and a perfect first for my autistic daughter.

NICE OUTSIDE. SMALL ENTRANCE. EXCITING.

Very exciting.

DARK RED? SMALL KIOSK WHERE YOU HAD TO PAY ON THE LEFT.'

The seats were comfortable.

'I seem to remember when it was all done out and looked super afterwards. Love the view down to the screen. Love the intimate layout. Cosy. Local.'

I remember it later had a great programme.

IT WAS COSY [...] SO NICE TO BE ABLE TO WALK TO A CINEMA, WE MADE THE MOST OF IT.

I THINK THERE WERE ABOUT THREE PEOPLE WATCHING THE FILM AND THAT INCLUDED ME.

THEY ALSO USED TO DO LIVE WRESTLING THERE. I REMEMBER BEING GUIDED TO YOUR SEAT BY A LADY WITH A TORCH.

COMFY SEATS

There was a computer fix-it place next to it and Raj was always standing outside.

MUCH AS I DO NOW; A WONDERFUL FACILITY IN ALTON SHOWING A WIDE VARIETY OF NEW RELEASES. ALSO WAS TOLD DEVELOPING THE BINGO HALL WOULD PAY FOR IMPROVEMENTS/BAR FOR THE CINEMA.

IT MEANT A LOT TO HAVE SOMEWHERE LOCAL, NOT PART OF A CHAIN. WE PREFER TO SUPPORT INDEPENDENT BUSINESSES.

IT WAS A VERY IMPORTANT PART OF LIFE. THERE WASN'T MUCH ELSE IN THE WAY OF ENTERTAINMENT.

IT FELT OLD FASHIONED BUT YOU COULD TELL IT WAS VERY WELL ESTABLISHED.

During the 50s and 60s, loads of clean seats and clean toilets.

It was quite busy, was a multi use building, having a disco on a Wednesday night as I remember and also wrestling used to take place there.

DID YOU GO TO SEE CHILDREN'S FILMS ON A SATURDAY AT THE PALACE?

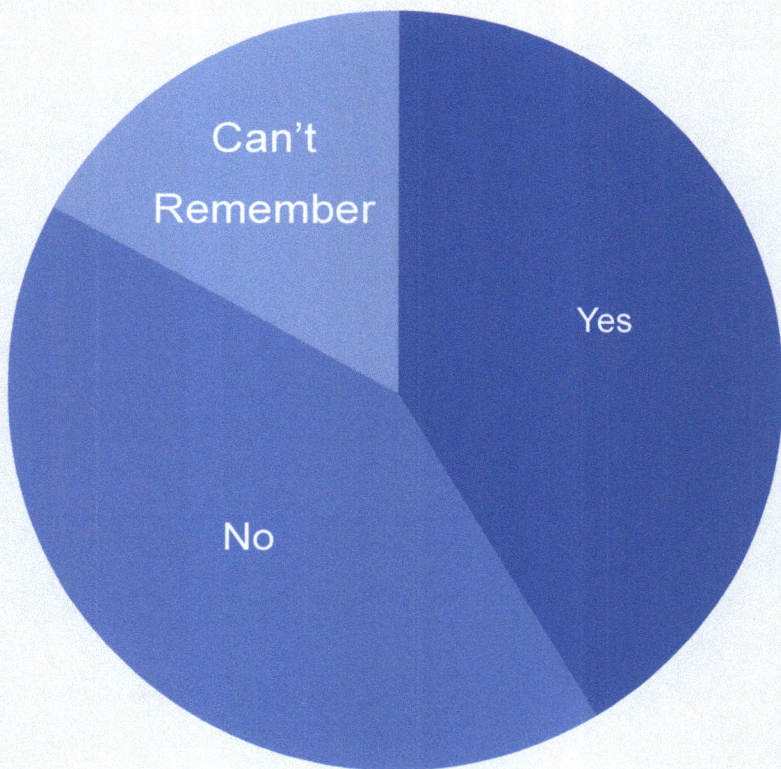

Can't Remember

Yes

No

WHO DID YOU GO TO THE PALACE CINEMA WITH?

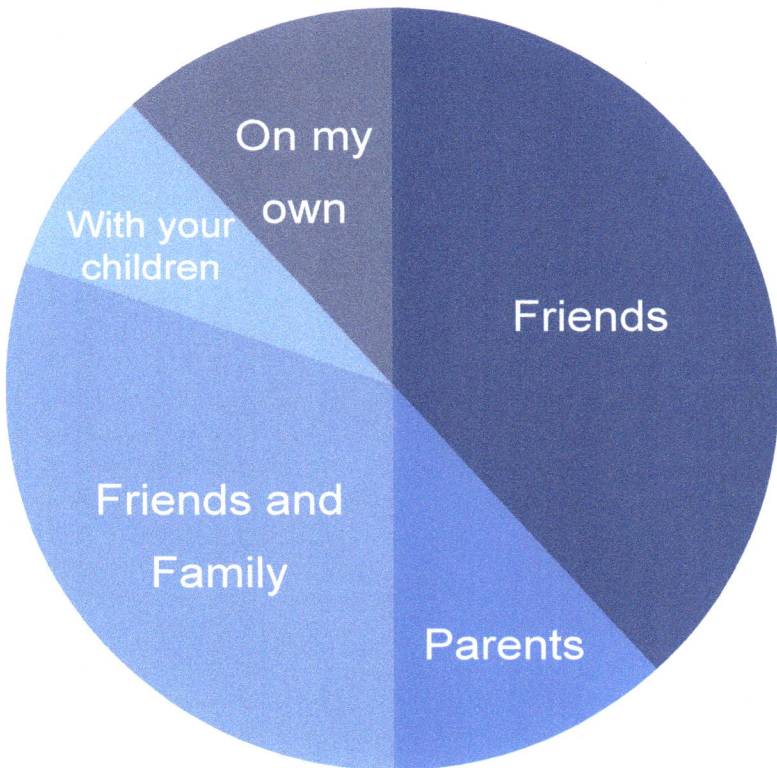

On my own

With your children

Friends

Friends and Family

Parents

DID YOU GO TO THE PALACE CINEMA AS A CHILD?

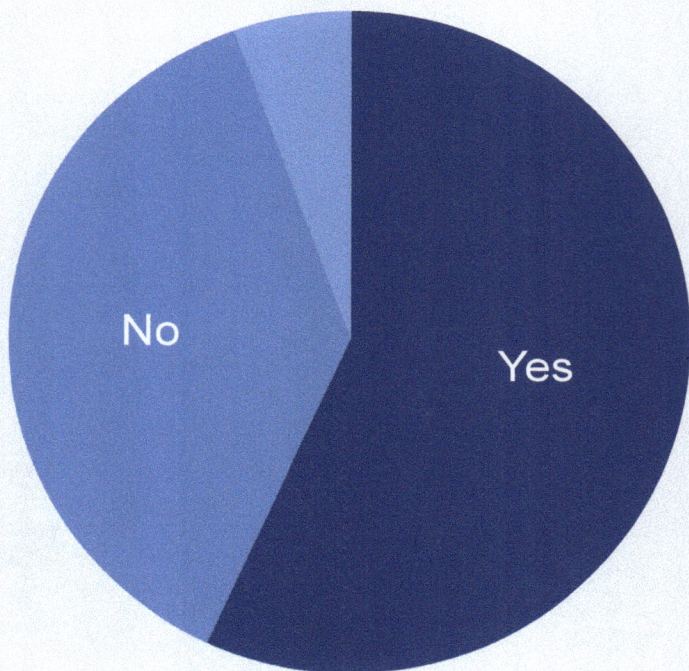

As a teenager

No

Yes

WHAT AGE WERE YOU?

6

11

5

From about 8

10

12

5

10

14
I think about 5 or 6

15

5–12 (12 is my current age)

14

From age 2 upwards

17–18

17 when first went 9

4

From age 4 or 5 I think

About 4–5 yrs old

17–maybe younger, but don't remember

10

COME ALONG AND

RECORD YOUR MEMORIES OF THE PALACE CINEMA

**19th November 2022 2-4pm
Alton Community Centre**

Come and share your memories
of the Palace and of cinema-going
in Alton for our Oral History Project

ALL WELCOME

Just turn up and have a chat with us.
memoriesofthepalace@gmail.com
@memoriesofthepalacecinemaalton

*'Record your memories of the Palace Cinema' flyer designed by Rebecca Slama.
Photo © Abbe Fletcher*

* GUILD OF OPTIMISTS *

Lois Leonard
Interview by Chris Stone
Memories of the Palace Cinema Launch
24th September 2022

Chris Stone: Talking to Lois Leonard about memories of the Alton Palace cinema, so many thanks for talking to us, Lois. What would perhaps be one of your favourite films that you've seen at the cinema?

Lois Leonard: With my friends, I watched the new Doctor Strange film *[Doctor Strange in the] Multiverse of Madness* and that was an entertaining experience. I think I'll remember that for a while.

C.S. Any particular reasons why it was entertaining?

L.L. Mostly because we tried to flip up seats while people were lying on them and flying marshmallow fights, they were interesting because we had the whole cinema to ourselves. It was very entertaining.

C.S. Very entertaining. You put in an awful lot of work, it's a shame that we can't actually see it as part of a radio interview, but a poster, Memories of the Palace Cinema, what was sort of your inspiration behind putting this together?

L.L. Part of the reason we moved to Alton in the first place was for the cinema and my mum, who organised this, has put her heart and soul into this so I thought I should put some of mine into it.

C.S. Nowadays, it's so easy to get a tablet or a phone and watch a film stream. Do you think it's better going to see a film at the cinema?

L.L. It's mostly the experience because some movies, you have to have that big screen and big sound to experience the sort of thrill of the cinema, really, but you can't get that on your flat screen or your phone and it would be such a shame to lose something that's given people that thrill for so many years, over 100 years.

C.S. Excellent, so many thanks for talking to us, Lois.

L.L. Thank you.

> '...SOME MOVIES, YOU HAVE TO HAVE THAT BIG SCREEN AND BIG SOUND TO EXPERIENCE THE SORT OF THRILL OF THE CINEMA...'

Palace Cinema show times and closure announcement from the Palace Cinema website, 2022.
Photo © Abbe Fletcher

*Lois Leonard interviewed by Chris Stone, 2022.
Photo © Abbe Fletcher*

*Memories of the Palace Cinema Poster by Lois Leonard, Alton, Hampshire, Launch event, 2022.
Photo © Abbe Fletcher*

DO YOU HAVE MEMORIES OF ANY SHENANIGANS FROM CHILDHOOD CINEMA VISITS?
WERE THEY QUIET SCREENINGS OR ROWDY? WERE THE CHILDREN ACCOMPANIED?

I took my younger brother to see *Wizard of Oz*, he was about 5 I would have been 7 or 8. He was frightened by the Tin Man I think and I had to take him out.

Went with school and friends or family. Busy but quiet during film.

It was quite a good atmosphere not noisy not quiet.

PERFECTLY FINE. I REMEMBER THE CINEMAS BEING FULL OF PEOPLE AND GETTING TO CHOSE WHERE YOU SAT ON THAT CHART BUT NOW THERE ARE LIKE LESS THEN 10 PEOPLE IN THE CINEMA AT ONCE.

When we went to see *Together* we went as a whole community from Thedden Grange, it's about a Swedish commune and there were some funny parallels, particularly the part where he makes two pieces of Lego out of wood for the kids to play with and then gives up. We could all identify and the Palace was full of our collective laughter and energy.

I went to see the new *Doctor Strange* movie with my friends, we had the big screen all to ourselves and there were a lot of flying marshmallows and M&Ms. We lay on four seats each and in the middle of the movie, creep up on them and flip the seats up or sit on them and the seats.

On the Saturday morning club it was just us kids and a lot of sugar filled sweets. It wasn't quiet it was a really fun morning.

ALWAYS QUIET SCREENINGS NEVER ROWDY

JUST CHILDREN... LOL

I WAS WITH MY FRIENDS WHEN WE WERE IN YEAR 7, WE WERE THE ONLY ONES THERE, IT WAS GREAT! WE LAUGHED A LOT.

We went on our own but sometimes with family

OFTEN HIT BY FLYING PEANUTS FROM ABOVE ! A BIT NOISY DURING THE INTERVAL :)

WE WERE DOING BREAKDANCING CLASSES AT THE DANCE STUDIO AT THE TIME AND WERE ABLE TO GET UP AND DANCE THROUGHOUT THE PERFORMANCE. REALLY FANTASTIC ENERGY.

ACCOMPANIED AND QUIET

MY SISTER WAS TOLD TO LEAVE THE CINEMA BECAUSE SHE WAS EATING FISH AND CHIPS.

NEW
CYCLE LANES
AHEAD

BINGO

PALACE

CINEMA

EVERY NIGHT NATIONAL & LINK GAME PLAYED

PALACE Cobbler   PALACE SOCIAL CLUB

Cinema   Stage

The Palace in 1990. Photo © Tony Cross

Alison White: My name's Alison White. I worked at the Palace Cinema in Alton between 1990 and 2003.

Abbe Fletcher: So, how did you start? Was the job advertised?

A.W. Mark, the previous owner to Raj, advertised the position of usherette. At the time, I was a stay-at-home Mum, but I still wanted to contribute. I thought I could go out in the evenings when my husband came home. I applied for the job. I went and met Mark at the cinema. I came home really excited, but Mark phoned later and said he'd offered the job to someone else. I was disappointed but thought, never mind, and didn't think any more of it.

The next day, he phoned back and said the lady who had taken the job had resigned. He asked if I would like to come in. I agreed and loved it. It was like it was meant to be.

I started at the box office; I would sell tickets for the cinema and bingo. At that time, in 1990, three people were working in the cinema on any particular evening. There would be a person in the box office, an usherette and a projectionist. I would sell the tickets, and then when the film started, I would go home.

Then the usherette left, and they decided to combine two jobs. So I would sell tickets and then during the intermission, between the trailers and the film, I'd go down to the front of the cinema with a tray around my neck and sell ice creams.

I'd been working there for probably about three years when the projectionist left. Mark asked me if I fancied learning how to show the film. I said I'd really like to. He was the one who taught me to be a projectionist. I'm grateful to him for that. He was the one who gave me the opportunity. And I remember thinking, 'Oh, you trust me with that?'

I was trained as the projectionist, and I remained doing so until 2003. I used to work three evenings a week. That's how it all started.

A.F. What did you like about being a projectionist?

A.W. I think seeing all the films. People loved me on their quiz team because if there was a round on current films, I knew them all! We were like family there. Everybody knew everyone else, and we all got on really well. It was a very small team, and I enjoyed that. I had a young family at home, and it was just so removed from my daily life that I was a different person. I know it's probably difficult for younger people to understand that because everybody works now when they have their family, but we didn't. I stayed at home with the children until they went to secondary school, which I absolutely loved, but I did like being myself in the evening.

'PEOPLE LOVED ME ON THEIR QUIZ TEAM BECAUSE IF THERE WAS A ROUND ON CURRENT FILMS, I KNEW THEM ALL!'

A.F. So, there were two screens then?

A.W. There were never two screens during the time I worked there. It was quite a while after I left that the second screen came. When I was there, the downstairs was bingo, which was really thriving. You could still see that the bingo hall had been a cinema as the floors at the sides sloped down, all the seats had been taken out and the tables put in for the bingo. There was a little bar on the left and the office on the right as you went in.

The bingo used to be full every night, and they would log into the national game at 9 pm. The national game was one that nearly all the bingo halls in the country were playing. The prize was a very large amount of cash. Occasionally, in the bingo, you would hear a crash from upstairs because there was a blockbuster showing.

A.F. So, the balcony. Can you tell me a bit about that?

A.W. The small cinema I knew was on the balcony of the original building. That was converted in the 1990s.

I never saw the cinema as it was originally downstairs. When the bingo was there, at the front, it still had the original stage curtains, which would have had the big screen behind it. There used to be outbuildings out there and I think that's where the flats are now.

A.F. Which year do you think you started being protectionist?

A.W. I went in 1990, so maybe 1993. I was the projectionist for about ten years.

A.F. Could you tell us about your typical day as a projectionist?

A.W. I worked Tuesday and Thursday evenings, and on a Saturday, I would show the matinée and the evening performance as well. I'd arrive about half an hour before the showing and lace the film up in the projector. I likened it to threading my sewing machine, it's very similar.

A.F. How many reels per film?

A.W. Roughly, about five or six. They'd come in quite small reels, and then on a Friday morning, I would go up to the cinema, and in the back room, I'd splice the films together and add the trailers.

You had to be very careful with the film because if you touched it, that mark would come up on the screen and it was crucial that the film never touched the floor because it would pick up the dust. You can see this in very old films; they show all the dust on the screen. But it did occasionally happen.

When you put the film on, you didn't have to constantly sit up in the projection box. You could go down into the auditorium to watch the film if you wanted to. But the only thing is if the film broke after it had gone through the projector, you would be unaware.

The only time it happened to me was very memorable. As we've got four children, it was very rare that my husband would have the opportunity to come to the cinema to meet me after the film so that we could go for a drink.

One evening, he came to meet me after a showing of the film *The Remains of the Day*. I went up to the projection box, and when I opened the door, the film was all over the floor, it must have broken near the beginning as it almost filled the projection box! My husband took one look and said, 'It's the Remains of the Film!' So, I had to spend all that evening putting the film back onto the reel.

At least in ten years, that was the only disaster I had ever experienced. I remember watching *Gremlins*, and suddenly, the film all burns up on the screen. I was down in the auditorium when it burnt up, and I thought, 'Oh my goodness!'. I ran up the steep stone steps to the projection box and the film was fine. Of course, it's the scene in *Gremlins* where they burn the film in the projection box! I was talking to one of the other projectionists and he said, 'Oh, that happened to me too!' I wondered how many projectionists all over the country had done the same thing.

For the performance, there was a definite sequence in which to do everything. Whilst people were coming in, we would have the lights on either side of the screen (called the walkers), the lights in the arch above the screen and the lights along the edge of the steps all on. And we'd have music playing.

Then, when I was about to start the film, I'd fade the music, fade the lights from the arch, turn the walkers off and then bring the shutter up for the film to come on whilst bringing the sound up on the film. Being a manual process, it can have its drawbacks. I remember once going to see *Apocalypse Now* in Putney. We watched the first half an hour with no dialogue, in total silence, because we thought that was how it was supposed to be. When someone finally spoke, we realized that the sound wasn't up.

A.F. How do the reels work? Do you have to change them often?

A.W. With the projector that we had; it would all be on one reel because we would have spliced the small reels together to go onto one massive reel. It would just run continually until the end. But it was a very old projector. I don't think they've got that at the cinema now. I haven't been up there for years; I think they've probably got cassettes now.

A.F. Do you remember the make of the projector?

A.W. I don't. But whilst working there, my family and I went to Cadbury's World. There was a projector in the museum there, and I was amazed to see that it was exactly the same as the one at the Palace. So it was pretty old. It's probably the original projector.

A.F. Did you ever take photos in the projection booth?

A.W. No, but you had to go out onto the flat roof to get into the projection booth. I went to the edge and took photos down the High Street. But I never took any inside.

A.F. Do you have any memories of particular films?

> 'I'D ARRIVE ABOUT HALF AN HOUR BEFORE THE SHOWING AND LACE THE FILM UP IN THE PROJECTOR. I LIKENED IT TO THREADING MY SEWING MACHINE, IT'S VERY SIMILAR.'

A.W. There are certain films that I think of fondly, like *Four Weddings and a Funeral*, *Shirley Valentine* or *The Full Monty*. For films like that, we would be full and have to turn people away. Those were the glory days.

A.F. So, did you watch films repeatedly?

A.W. It would depend on the film, and sometimes, if they weren't my kind of film, I would take a book to read in the projection box. *The Full Monty* was brilliant; I would watch it every night because I knew when the laughs were coming, and rather than watching the film, I would watch the audience and wait for them to erupt in laughter. Especially the scene in the job centre when they all start dancing. I still love that scene now when I watch it at home.

Certain films I would watch over again and others I wouldn't watch at all. For every film, I'd have to sit there until the end and there would always be people – and I'm actually one of those people now – that sit to the bitter end to see where it was filmed.

So, to while away the time of the credits, I started a little game with myself. I would try to find all my family's Christian names in the titles. There were only a couple of films where I got all our names, but it just passed the time.

A.F. A projectionist's game. Did you notice how films have changed over the thirteen years you worked there?

A.W. Yes, I think nowadays there are more blockbusters. I think there were a lot more British film then. That period was a sort of British Revival of films. Because Farnham didn't have a cinema and neither did Winchester, we would be showing films like that to try and attract those people.

'I SAW THE WRITING WAS ON THE WALL. NOW, IT'S ALL DIGITAL, SO THE ART OF PROJECTING IS ALL BUT LOST.'

A.F. So what kind of films would attract people?

A.W. Historical dramas like *Pride and Prejudice*. All the classics, although we showed all the new films as well.

A.F. So it was a repertory cinema then in terms of picking and programming?

A.W. Yes.

A.F. Who programmed the films?

A.W. The owner would choose the film.

A.F. Having an active part in the screening of the films certainly provided the expertise that comes with being a projectionist.

A.W. Having started as an usherette, by the end, cutbacks meant that I did everything in the evening. I'd sell the tickets and ice creams at the box office because the usherette had become a thing of the past, then I'd go and start the film and see everyone out at the end. People used to think it was hilarious that I did the whole thing.

A.F. A one-woman show! Did you lock up?

A.W. Yes, put the alarms on and locked up. That was probably from about 2000 onwards.

A.F. What was the worst part of your job?

A.W. If it was a long film that I didn't like and I had to be there three or four nights a week, it could get boring, especially if the credits were long. It didn't happen very often, to be fair, but that was the worst part. And the credits are so long now because even the person in the hot dog stall seems to get a mention!

A.F. Were you the first female projectionist there?

A.W. I wouldn't like to say something categorically because I don't know all the other projectionists, but I guess it's possible I was.

A.F. Did you get attention for that, or was it not a big deal?

A.W. It was no big deal at the cinema. But if people asked me, 'What do you do?' they were astounded and still are. When Raj came, I suppose he just accepted it; he never seemed to think it was strange. It was a perfect job for me because it fitted in with my family.

But saying that, the pay was awful, which is part of why I left because I really had to start earning a bit more money. I really didn't want to leave, but I had to. Before I had children, I worked in microbiology – so I went back to lab work.

A.F. That's amazing.

A.W. I've never thought of myself as being interesting. It's just a different age. It's all very different now. Shortly after I left, The Vue Cinema in Basingstoke opened. My son had the opportunity through his job to have a 'behind-the-scenes' look before it opened.

I was amazed when he explained the projection box, which was just one long room with several projectors in a line, each facing a different cinema screen. At that time, the films were on video cassettes.

This meant they only needed one projectionist to slot all the videos in and press the buttons. I saw the writing was on the wall. Now, it's all digital, so the art of projecting is all but lost.

A.F. You must know what you're doing with projectors. Do you have any stories of things that happened when lacing them up?

A.W. When everyone had left the building, we would put the bright strip lights on for cleaning. One night after the film, when we put the strip lights up, we discovered a man slumped in front of his seat. He was surrounded by beer bottles and had passed out. There were two of us at the time, and we just couldn't wake him up. Luckily, at that time, the police station was still over the road, so I ran across there, and two burly policemen came and dragged him out. They put him in the cells for the night to sleep it off.

As it was a local cinema, we had regulars. I still see them around the town now. I wouldn't know their names, but they say hello as we recognise each other from the cinema because they came every week.

A.F. You have a great memory. Has Alton changed a lot?

A.W. It's changed an awful lot – probably about double the size. The core of Alton is still there, and we still love living here. We're both retired now and thought about moving away, but we've got our friends here and the community. I think there's evidence of the community spirit in the project that you're doing.

A.F. That's lovely. Do you still go to the cinema?

A.W. Yes, we do. But it needs to be a film we really want to see. We wouldn't go just for an evening out. We went to see *Downton*

Abbey recently, which we loved. We watch films at home more now. We'll sometimes cruise through Netflix, but we quite often buy DVDs in charity shops. We were looking for *Notting Hill* and thought that would be on Netflix, but it wasn't. But then we found it in a charity shop.

A.F. And it's cheap. But cinema-going, I think it's something you said about being in a space with other people.

A.W. *The Full Monty* is the only film that got a standing ovation everynight. In the end, everybody just clapped and stood up, and I'd never seen it before in a cinema. Or since.

A.F. Wow. Yes, it is that uniting everyone. How do you think the Palace has managed to stay open so long?

A.W. I just don't know. My knowledge sort of stopped in 2003, really. It had a regular clientele; people would go every week. That 'we're just going to see whatever's on' attitude. But that's part of another time.

> 'THE FULL MONTY IS THE ONLY FILM THAT GOT A STANDING OVATION EVERY NIGHT ... I'D NEVER SEEN IT BEFORE IN A CINEMA. OR SINCE.'

A.F. Yes, as a kind of habitual, regular thing. Just going to the pictures. You've mentioned a bit about this project with collecting the memories, but what are your thoughts about it?

A.W. I think it's lovely, I really do. Because as you said, it will be an historical record. In years to come, people will move into the town and never even realise there had been a cinema here.

A.F. Lastly, when you left, did you get a send-off, or was it quite low-key?

A.W. [Laughs] No, just 'bye'.

A.F. Did you continue to go to the cinema as a punter?

A.W. Not very often. I found it too hard and too sad, really.

A.F. Why was that?

A.W. Because I loved it so much. We have been back, but not regularly.

A.F. Do you have any thoughts on the Palace closing?

A.W. Yes, I'm very sad about it, really sad. If there was anything that could be done to keep it going…

A.F. Thank you very much for talking to me and sharing your memories.

'I THINK THERE'S EVIDENCE OF THE COMMUNITY SPIRIT IN THE PROJECT THAT YOU'RE DOING.'

The Palace Cinema's 'Full House' sign. Photo © Raj Jeyasingam

Which films did you see?

Finding Your Feet

Military Wives

Fisherman's Friends

KRAMER VS. KRAMER

SUPERMAN

Ballerina

House of Gucci

Wizard of Oz

MOANA

Breakdance

FROZEN

Roy Rogers

THE BAD GUYS

Grease

LORD OF THE RINGS

The Matrix

Bambi

Together

Tarzan

La Traviata

PADDINGTON 2

See How They Run

Dune

Lion King

Mamma Mia

AVENGERS INFINITY WAR

INDIANA
JONES AND THE LAST CRUSADE

DESERT SONG

The Secret Life of

PETS

Walking on Sunshine

17

SONIC THE HEDGEHOG

Me Before You

Mamma Mia: Here We Go Again

AGAIN

Murder on the Orient Express

STAR WARS

Off the Rails

The Duke

Pitch Perfect

The Book Club

Fame

MACBETH

Bridget Jones

West Side Story

American

Jungle Book

Hustle

JURASSIC PARK

Annie

The

High

Terminator

Maggie's Plan

SNOW WHITE

School

The Lucky One

Musical

The Shape of Water

Magic Mike

Fifty Shades of Grey

Palace Cinema Second Screen, 2011, Alton, Hampshire. Photo by © Mick Collins.

Palace Cinema Large Screen, 2011, Alton, Hampshire. Photo by © Mick Collins.

Simon Wood
Audio Engineer/Producer and owner of
Dubmaster Studios, Alton
20th October 2022

Simon Wood: My name's Simon Wood. I've lived in Alton all my life, and I was a regular cinema-goer when I was a kid. I used to go every week.

Abbe Fletcher: Do you remember your first visit [to the Palace cinema]?

S.W. Well, all the visits were the same, because every time I went, it seemed like the same show. [chuckles] I think it was the fact that we got free sweets, or the sweets were included. I'm pretty sure it was sixpence to get in, and it included something like a Jamboree bag of sweets.

Kat Guenioui: What decade are we talking about?

S.W. That'd be 1960s. I reckon probably when I was eight years old, so 1967, 1968.

A.F. Do you remember what the films were?

S.W. I think we saw things like *Casey Jones*, but that was also on TV, so I'm not so sure. I think *The Lone Ranger* was a regular series, and there was the guy who does the Z with a sword-

K.G. *[The Mask of] Zorro*?

S.W. *[The Mask of] Zorro*, but I'm not sure about that either. What I really remember is the cartoons, I just wanted short laughs. I've got a very short attention span, so there was stuff like – I'm not sure if it was *Tom and Jerry*, but it was that sort of thing. Cartoons were the highlight for me.

A.F. When you were little, did you going to the cinema on a Saturday?

63

S.W. Yes, it was Saturday Morning Cinema Club.

A.F. Do you remember what it was like inside at that time?

S.W. Yes, I remember exactly what it was like. I think it was still probably completely original in the 1960s. There were Art Deco panels on the side, which I think might've had some lighting in them. The beautiful Art Deco ceiling was reflected as well. I think there might have been chandeliers hanging from the Art Deco sections. The stage looked great. It was only about six feet deep to the screen, I think, but they still used to pull people up on there. If it was your birthday, you were pulled up on stage.

A.F. Did that happen to you?

S.W. I was so shy, I might not have admitted it was my birthday, I don't remember going up on stage. Most of the people I've talked to say, 'Do you remember the birthdays?' I do remember people going up on stage for their birthdays.

A.F. Who did you go with at that time?

'I'M PRETTY SURE IT WAS SIXPENCE TO GET IN, AND IT INCLUDED SOMETHING LIKE A JAMBOREE BAG OF SWEETS.'

S.W. I can't remember if I went on my own. This was back in the time when I used to go to infant school on my own and I think I probably went to the cinema on my own. I may have gone with my sister, but I think I went on my own.

A.F. Were your mates there?

S.W. I think every kid from Alton was at the cinema. That was the place to be on Saturday mornings.

A.F. That's fantastic. Do you remember when you were a teenager?

S.W. What I remember mostly about the cinema when I was a teenager, getting a bit spotty, were the discos. I think it was Friday nights. They ended up having trouble there with lads from other towns coming in, and it got a bit rough, so I think that's what stopped it. The discos: they inspired me, because I've ended up as a sound engineer, and I remember the guy who ran those discos. He had really big speakers, and that blew me away. That's one of the things that got me into sound, but the cinema also got me into sound and light. That's what inspired me when I was a kid. That was probably more interesting to me than what was on the screen. The sound, the environment, the lighting, it had an impact on me. That's probably why I do what I do.

A.F. That's wonderful. Did you go to the cinema as a teenager?

S.W. I would've done. I can't remember what sort of films we went to see. They would've been the blockbusters at the time, that's what you went to the cinema for. I'm sure we went quite regularly, but it tailed off as the cinema deteriorated. I think the last time I sat in that cinema was probably three years ago, pre-Covid, and I was probably going once, twice a year maybe. It's really sad, but if you've got a comfortable setup at home, you wouldn't want to sit in a cinema that's deteriorating. For me, the disaster was when it was converted to the upstairs balcony section only as the main screen, because it was an amazing cinema. I think it seated around 450 people, which was big for a little town like this.

A.F. Was it quite full in terms of capacity?

S.W. On a blockbuster movie it would be full, yes. You'd queue up outside – I remember being in the queue, getting nervous, thinking 'Are we going to actually get in?'. I think we always did get in; it would be pretty full.

A.F. That's great to hear. That conversion happened in the 1990s?

S.W. I can't remember when it happened. I think it was a gradual process. They were running bingo there with the conventional seating still in.

Then when bingo got really popular, I guess they thought they could make more money from this than films in the main auditorium. They took the seating out. It really upset me. I think it ended up with a level floor, they took the rake out and everything.

A.F. When would that have been do you think?

S.W. Early 1990s probably, I don't remember sitting in the downstairs screen to watch a film for a long time. I can't remember being in there, so I would've thought it was early 1990s that they lost that. There was a time when you went to see a film and you could see that bingo also took place there. I think there was a lectern area where the bingo caller would be, and the raked seating was still there. They were doing both at the same time for a while.

'THE SOUND, THE ENVIRONMENT, THE LIGHTING, IT HAD AN IMPACT ON ME.'

A.F. Then the conversion of the bingo hall into flats in 2014-

S.W. Yes, I didn't even know that happened. I didn't believe it. I thought, 'There's no way.' I actually went to have a look because I couldn't believe it. They chopped a bit off the back. That was a shame, because I thought that means it can never be restored back to how it was.

K.G. I think a few months ago, we sort of lost hope with saving the cinema. That's why we put more energy into this project to try and preserve the memories at least.

S.W. I would also say that they didn't make much of a noise about the planning, because I think a lot of people would've jumped up and said, 'Hang on a minute. I never knew anything about planning to demolish part of it.' I think I would have put my signature somewhere if I'd known.

Going back to how it influenced me when I was a kid: one of the things that was a disaster is when they started knocking out bits of the Art Deco stuff. The first thing they did, when they started doing the discos there, is put in these huge colourful Perspex panels, boxes on the wall with lighting in them. I thought that was fantastic, at the time. Now, I think, 'Oh, what a shame.' That was the beginning of the decor being knocked around; when the disco sort of adapted to put some clever, funky, typical 1970s lighting in.

That would've been the late 1970s when they were doing the discos. That influenced me because I went and built the same in my bedroom at home. [laughs] I had funky lighting in my bedroom. I thought, 'That's cool,' but it was awful.

I doubt in the modern world whether the sound was very good, but it was probably the best I'd heard then. I come from a pretty working-class family, so we didn't travel to other towns, other cinemas. That was the only cinema I went to. The sound was great. My dad had a good Hi-Fi, but the sound at the cinema was better. That definitely is something I wanted to replicate, so I built speakers and stuff when I was a kid and just got stuck in.

A.F. In terms of shifting habits or viewing habits, it's very much gone to individual at home with your own setup. That idea of being out in a big space with big sound, and the sound is sometimes more important than the image.

> ## 'THE SOUND IS SOMETIMES MORE IMPORTANT THAN THE IMAGE.'

S.W. It was incredibly important to me. I can't sit in a cinema that hasn't got great sound. It'd be one of the main criticisms of the existing cinema. It's got okay sound, but it doesn't fill the room. If you're going to go and see a film that's got an important soundtrack, that's not the place to see it.

A.F. You don't know what kind of setup they have?

'THAT'S THE SORT OF THING YOU REMEMBER WHEN YOU'RE A KID, THE GLOW ON THE ICE CREAM LADY'S FACE.'

S.W. No idea. It'll be just a basic surround system, with three channels behind the screen. You have a channel in the middle so that dialogue always sounds like it comes from the middle, otherwise it's off.

It's a bit off if they do it in stereo, so they have a center channel for the majority of the dialogue, and then two more speakers behind, at the back of the screen, at the side. That's the main stereo image and the surround, but in modern cinemas you can have Dolby Atmos [which] is dozens of channels of surround, and they all can be individually addressed, so you can put a sound anywhere in the theater really.

A.F. Do you know anything about the projectors?

S.W. No. I'm pretty sure they've got digital projection now, and it's okay. It does mean you don't have to stop halfway through the film like they did when we were kids.

That was the intermission, that was to change the reel, and that's when the ice cream lady came out. That's another highlight, and it's something that I think people miss, is a break in the middle. Especially if you're sitting through a three-hour film, a break is quite welcome.

They'd always sell ice cream up to the start of the film. They would stand there during the commercials with a little tray lit with a dim light reflected upward lighting their face. That's the sort of thing you remember when you're a kid, the glow on the ice cream lady's face. Then they'd come out again at the intermission.

A.F. What kind of ice cream?

S.W. Little tubs. I think it was ice lollies and ice cream tubs. And they were melting by the time you got back to your seat. [laughs]

K.G. Lots of people have said about things being thrown around during the Saturday morning kids' club-

S.W. There were things thrown, yes. I don't remember food being thrown, but enough of it spilled on the floor. Nothing too aggressive. A little bit of cardboard would hit you on the back of the head, and some sniggering behind you.

Another thing I remember, not for the children's cinema club, but if you went to see a film, there was always this guy who seemed to be in every film smoking. They smoked in the cinema back then. Instead of drawing on his cigarette all the time, he would quite often blow on it to create sparks, I think it was to make us laugh. You'd be in a dark room, and occasionally, you'd see these sparks flying out in front of this guy. A couple of friends remember it as well, but he seemed to be in every film. [laughs]

A.F. We've heard of kids sitting on top of the balcony dropping stuff, and it almost seemed to be a class divide; the people who had more money sat upstairs.

S.W. Yes, it was definitely more expensive up top, we would rarely sit up top. I can't remember the prices, but I think if you paid sixpence downstairs, you paid something like half a crown upstairs. Sixpence is two and a half pence, I think, so half a crown is double that, so five pence upstairs, double the price.

A.F. You could see two films for that. In the 1970s, do you remember how much it was to get into the discos or anything like that?

S.W. No, I don't.

K.G. Did they have a bar in there?

S.W. No, because some people were under 16. I think you could buy drinks, pop, but I'm pretty sure there was no bar. I do remember an almighty fight outside in the street that I think sparked the end of the discos.

K.G. I was just going to ask how you managed to have a disco. What did they do with the seats? Or was there plenty of room?

S.W. I think the seats remained in. I think they made space down at the front. A fair amount of space, actually. I think they took out a part of the middle section to produce a square, so it was probably about a 10-meter by 10-meter square area. Everyone who was looking for a partner would be hanging around up in the seated area, but the dancing was down in the middle. There wasn't a lot of dancing though. [laughter]

A.F. Do you remember what kind of music was playing?

S.W. Yes, 1970s funk and soul. Good stuff.

A.F. What else was there to do in Alton for young people at that time?

S.W. Not much. If you were still of school age, we had the youth club at the school which opened in the evenings. They had discos.

A.F. Which school was that?

S.W. Amery Hill. When you were much younger, you would've automatically gone to Sunday school, whether you were a religious family or not. They were more like a club. There wasn't an awful lot for kids to do. When we were teenagers, we hung out in a couple of cafes in the town. A cafe called The Rendezvous, which is probably around about where the Newbury is now. That was a typical cafe at the front with a counter down one side. You could go and get a cup of coffee or whatever, and at the back it had pinball machines. That's where me and the lads were, on the pinball machines. There wasn't a lot, [for kids to do]. Not until you were old enough to go to a pub.

A.F. There were lots of pubs around there at that time.

S.W. A lot, yes. I think when I was in my late teens, there were probably twenty-two, twenty-three pubs. Yes. A pub crawl was difficult. [laughter]

A.F. Were there motorbikes?

S.W. We had our local Hell's Angels group. We knew some of them. You wanted to stay on the right side of them. We had bikes, some of [my mates] were serious bike enthusiasts and would rebuild British bikes, so we were into bikes as well. We loved our bikes.

A.F. What do you think about closing the cinema? What are your thoughts?

> 'I CAN HARDLY REMEMBER THE FILMS I WENT TO SEE BECAUSE I WOULD BE JUST LOOKING AROUND THE BUILDING STARING WIDE-EYED AT LIGHTS AND SOUND.'

S.W. I think it's awful that it's closing. It needs to be more than a cinema. It needs to be a place where people want to go for an experience, not just the film. Because you can see just the film at home, and you don't even have to wait long for films to be available online. I think unless cinemas do something different, they're going to have a tough time. Having said that, a new one opened last week in Woking with nine screens, I think (Nova Cinema).

It can still be done, but I don't know how it's made to work. If you go to the Vue, sometimes it's pretty full. They've taken out fifty per cent of the seats to put the big recliners in, so that must have a big impact, and they didn't seem to put the prices up massively, but we'll go there quite often. We sat in there and watched a great film with maybe ten people in there. How it pays, I don't know, I've not been to an Everyman yet. That's what we need to do with some of the small cinemas. Single-screen cinemas need to be an experience rather than just the film.

A.F. It's lovely to hear about the influence of the Palace on your chosen career.

S.W. I thought it might be a different angle, yes, not just the films. In fact, it's crazy, I can hardly remember the films I went to see because I would be just looking around the building staring wide-eyed at lights and sound.

That's what I remember. I'm sure I did watch the films, but that's not my memory – it was the immersive experience. All my life, I've tried to replicate that. At home, before I became a sound engineer, I would have decent sound. We never had any money, so I built everything. That's how I learnt to do what I do. I had to make everything because I couldn't afford to buy it, so it was an education for me.

K.G. It's lovely to think of that little cinema inspiring you in your career. That's really nice, and it must have been the same for other people I think, in different ways.

A.F. Well, that's just wonderful. Thank you so much. That just really makes it all feel so worth it and just really fascinating, so thank you for taking the time to talking to us.

S.W. You're welcome.

'IT'S LOVELY TO HEAR ABOUT THE INFLUENCE OF THE PALACE ON YOUR CHOSEN CAREER. '

Films alongside Bingo: Palace Cinema Advert in the Alton Gazette, 11th September 1969, Alton Library.
Photo by © Mick Collins.

Bingo at the Palace Cinema, 1986 (prior to its reopening as a Cinema in 1989). Photo © Tony Cross

WHICH FILMS WERE YOUR FAVOURITES AND WHO WERE YOUR FAVOURITE FILM STARS?

GLENDA JACKSON

Gordon MacRae and Shirley Jones

Rain Man

All of the above, Bill Nighy, Eddie Redmayne, Cate Blanchett, Benedict Cumberbatch

The Matrix

My favourite movie stars were very old when I was born, such as: Harrison Ford, Leonardo di Caprio (my nickname in school), Samuel L. Jackson, Sean Connery, Keanu Reeves, Michael Caine among others

LORD OF THE RINGS

ANNIE AND GREASE

I have many favourite films and film stars! Cinema films are always the best memories

DUSTIN HOFFMAN

I just like the cinema, it feels like a treat to watch a film, in the dark, no distractions

The King and I with
Yule Brinner

Meryl Streep

WHERE

THE

CRAWDADS

SING

I loved watching *Paddington* with my son at The Palace. The cinema was packed. His friends had wanted to go too, but missed out on getting places as it was full, so their mum had to drive to Basingstoke and we all met up afterwards to chat about the film. It was great having a local cinema when my son was young (he's now only 13), we used to go quite often

COWBOY AND ADVENTURE

Dwayne Johnson
in *Jungle Cruise*. **I**
liked the Marvel
films

So many great movies and stars

All good for different

reasons. Mainly

enjoyed watching my

children enjoy the kids

films

CAROUSEL AND *OLD YELLER*

SONIC
THE HEDGEHOG

MOANA

Schindler's
List

Stairs to street level from the Box Office, 2022.
Photo © Abbe Fletcher.

Alton Second Hand Books established 1989, right, across the road from the Palace Cinema.
Photo © Abbe Fletcher

Joan Andrews
Interview by Abbe Fletcher
2nd November 2022

Joan Andrews: My name is Joan Andrews. I started working at the cinema, probably in the middle of the '80s. There was an advert in the local paper asking for an accountant to work evenings, which I applied for, and it turned out that I had to work out the bingo prizes and then I would go down and mark the prize amount on the blackboard which was on the stage.

Some days, it was bingo and some days, cinema, so it was still the cinema seats. There were quite a few games, and that's really all I had to do.

The owner was Mark Eaton, he liked staff to wear a kind of uniform. I wore a black skirt, a white top, and if it was cold, which it usually was, a black cardigan. In those days, everybody could smoke, which they did. When you went home, you had to change and wash everything, particularly the wool cardigan.

There were quite a few of us helping out, I did that for quite a few years. The balcony was there at that time, I don't think it was changed until Raj took over. Raj said that when he took over, Mark gave him three years.

Abbe Fletcher: Did you go to the cinema back then?

J.A. Yes, Stan and I, we went regularly. We'd meet up [with friends] and go as a foursome. I've been to the cinema lots of times.

A.F. Do you remember what it was like when you were working at the Bingo? What was the decor like?

J.A. As I said, it hadn't altered. There was somebody selling ice creams and things like that.

A.F. When did you come to the bookshop [Alton Secondhand Books on Normandy Street, opposite the Palace Cinema]?

J.A. Here, I think we've been here twenty years.

A.F. What do you think about the cinema closing?

J.A. I have to say, since Covid, I probably haven't noticed. Before that, we used to get a lot of trade from the cinema, particularly the afternoon one. People used to come in and browse here before they went in. It's surprising how Covid has changed everything.

A.F. Yes. That's what's great about the cinema in terms of going to see a film, the latest release, whatever, in public with other people you don't know, laughing at the same moments or crying, sniffing at the same bits.

J.A. I can always remember one particular film. That's not so long ago, *Gone Girl*.

J.A. I'd read the book. Stan hadn't read it and he said, 'Well, shall we go?' I can remember the end when she just gets away with it. Everybody in the audience went [gasps].

A.F. That's what cinema can do. It's a shared experience. Thank you so much for this, Joan, it's been lovely to hear your memories.

> 'PEOPLE USED TO COME IN AND BROWSE HERE BEFORE THEY WENT IN. IT'S SURPRISING HOW COVID HAS CHANGED EVERYTHING.'

Palace Cinema bar and refreshments counter, 2011. Photo by © Mick Collins

Palace Cinema Bingo Hall, 2011, Alton, Hampshire. Photo by © Mick Collins.

HAVE YOU
BEEN TO THE
PALACE CINEMA
IN THE RUN UP TO
IT CLOSING IN 2022?

YES
50%

NO
41.2%

If so which films did you see?

TICKET to PARADISE

TOP GUN MAVERICK

OFF THE RAILS

The Secret Life of PETS

DOWNTON ABBEY

minions RISE OF GRU

FREE GUY

HOUSE OF GUCCI

FISHERMAN'S FRIENDS 2

WHERE THE CRAWDADS SING

ELVIS

DEATH ON THE NILE

SONIC THE HEDGEHOG

JUNGLE CRUISE

SUPER PETS

The Palace Cinema in Alton, Hampshire, July 2022.
Photo © Abbe Fletcher

Ellora Sutton
Interview by Abbe Fletcher
8th December 2022

Abbe Fletcher: Hi Ellora, thank you for talking to me about the Palace Cinema. Have you always lived in Alton or nearby?

Ellora Sutton: Yes. So I live in Kingsley very close to Alton. My family have always lived here.

A.F. Could you tell us a bit about your first memories of the Palace Cinema?

E.S. My first encounter wouldn't necessarily have been me actually going there, as my mum was a bingo caller at the Palace Cinema. I was very small, and my uncle was a projectionist at the Palace. He loved it because it meant he could watch the latest *Star Wars* film, just over and over again. When my mum applied for a job there, she was hoping that she would get to be a projectionist because, I think, *Pretty Woman* had just come out or something like that. It was a film that she really liked, and I think she had this fantasy of being able to watch it over and over again. She got a job as a bingo caller, and I was a very clingy child, and I used to resent it whenever my mum had to go and work at the bingo hall. That was my first encounter with the Palace Cinema as, sort of taking my mother away in the evenings.

But my actual first time going to the Palace Cinema was when Disney's *Tarzan* came out. I must have been three or four. The reason I wanted to go wasn't because I wanted to see *Tarzan*. It's because I wanted to go and see my uncle, and I was told he'd be running the projection. So I went with my mum to see *Tarzan*, but in my mind, I was going to see my uncle.

I get there, and I realize pretty quickly that I'm not going to get to hang out with uncle Jake. Within the first few minutes of the film, I start throwing a massive tantrum and have to get taken out of the cinema.

A.F. So your uncle, is that your mum's brother?

E.S. Yes. He worked there, and then he moved away and got a job at the Lighthouse in Poole, which is a sort of arts centre where they have a theatre and a cinema. I think it helped that he'd had this projectionist job [at the Palace Cinema] because he went into a technician's role there and is still there.

My next earliest memory of the Palace is going to see the first Harry Potter film. Again, I went with my mum and her godson, who's quite a bit older than me, and I was so little sitting on those fold-out chairs. I had to sit in the middle and they had to have one hand on each side of the seat to stop it from folding up and swallowing me up. I remember that. And before the film started, there were these disco lights projecting onto the white wall behind. And I always used to love sitting and watching them. To me was a really exciting moment when you sat and watched the disco lights before the film started.

'TO ME WAS A REALLY EXCITING MOMENT WHEN YOU SAT AND WATCHED THE DISCO LIGHTS BEFORE THE FILM STARTED.'

A.F. Would this be when it was two screens or one, do you think?

E.S. That would have been when it was one screen because I remember when the second screen was put in very vaguely. But I don't know if I remember being told about it, so just to give you an idea of how old, I'm 25. So my memories of my mum working there are from the late 1990s to early 2000s, I'd say.

It's interesting because when you went, it wasn't just to see a film, but to have an experience. [The lights] made it a very exciting thing. I went to see the Disney film *Cars*, and I remember running down that alleyway after the film, pretending to be a Lightning McQueen sports car.

A.F. That's great. Do you remember how full it was at those times?

E.S. The only time it ever felt busy was when I went to see *Charlotte's Web*, and that was the only time we had to book. Other than that, it always felt fairly empty in there. I can never remember going in those years and it being particularly busy.

But not that long ago, I went to see a live broadcast of *The Nutcracker* from the Royal Ballet there. I went with my nan, and it would have been in December 2017 or maybe 2016. That was really busy. I don't think they had a single empty seat for that, and that [gave] this sense of community and coming together because going to cinema is a shared experience. It's a shared cultural exchange. I've never been a massive cinemagoer, partly because I live in Kingsley and I don't drive. But also because I'm a bit of a homebody. But when I do go to the cinema, it is usually to see something I really want to see or something that I feel will be a cultural experience. And being in the venue of a cinema [will] add to [the experience], such as a live broadcast from the Royal Ballet or those big films like *Les Misérables*, for example.

A.F. Yes, it's the idea of the shared experience. It feels like that's disappearing from our culture in terms of getting us out of our homes. I wonder how cinema is faring after Covid in terms of getting together.

E.S. Yes, I must say that I haven't been to the cinema since the pandemic. The last time I went to cinema, was at the Palace, and it was to see the latest adaptation of *Emma* with Anya Taylor-Joy. I loved it. I think that was one of those occasions where seeing the film in the cinema added to it because there's this scene in *Emma* where the heroine, Emma, is a bit of a brat, but she's usually well-meaning. But she said something really quite cutting to another character called Miss Bates, an older woman. But when Emma said this really cutting thing to Miss Bates – played by Miranda Hart in the film – the entire cinema gasped, and I gasped. I don't think I would have had the same reaction watching it at home. But when you're there, and you're sharing it, you almost feel like you have to have an outward reaction because you want the rest of the cinema to know that you're reacting in an emotionally appropriate way.

That reminds me a little bit of when I went to see *War Horse* there with one of my friends. So I was in year ten or year eleven, and there's this harrowing scene where the horse is tangled up in barbed wire in the trenches, and everyone in the cinemas is almost crying; I was sad, too, and I think my friend could tell, and he kept trying to make me laugh. And I did laugh. And I [thought], 'It looks like I'm laughing at this horse in pain'. The enhanced emotional stakes, because you're there to watch a performance, but then sat in the audience, you become part of the performance.

A.F. That's brilliant. I think you're absolutely right. To have this communal experience where people laugh or gasp at the same moment, and you feel like you're part of something and that you're experiencing it together. Yes, that's really a strength of the cinema. It's lovely that you mention an Austen adaptation as the final film that you saw in Alton. So, was your uncle still projecting at that point, or had he left by then?

E.S. He'd left quite a long time ago. I would say the early 2000s.

A.F. We've interviewed a projectionist from around this period, and she was quite interesting to hear about in terms of the projectionist's point of view. She was saying that the credits are just getting longer and longer.

E.S. Yes. I think Raj was quite a late adapter of digital projection. I remember going to see the third *Pirates of the Caribbean* film. I begged to go and see it on a school night – I was in primary school at the time. I was allowed to go with my mum, and it was such a long film that they had to put an intermission in to change over the film canisters. I'd never experienced that before. I don't think I've experienced it since, but they were still using real film rather than digital. It's a bit like listening to vinyl rather than a CD, it had crackles in it.

So my uncle wasn't working there when Raj switched to digital, but he called my uncle and asked him for advice on swapping over to digital. That would have been the late 2000s, I think.

A.F. You wrote in your questionnaire that Butterkist was your snack of choice.

E.S. Yes, the toffee popcorn. I love that. I'm sure the people sitting around me hated it cause it's the crunch, isn't it?

A.F. Yes, exactly. I'm a big popcorn fan in the cinema too. I'm reading people's responses, and it's popular. But I'm also reading other oral histories of cinema-going – in particular a book that's just come out looking at British Cinema going in the 60s [Cinema Memories: A People's History of Cinema-going in 1960s Britain by Melvyn Stokes, Matthew Jones and Emma Pett, BFI 2022]. Popcorn was not as popular then; it's seen as American.

E.S. In America, I know they have it with melted butter, which sounds amazing.

> '...YOU'RE THERE TO WATCH A PERFORMANCE, BUT THEN SAT IN THE AUDIENCE, YOU BECOME PART OF THE PERFORMANCE.'

A.F. So, did you go to the bingo with your mum when she was working there?

E.S. Once, obviously, it wasn't for kids, but one time, she did take me with her, and that was really exciting for me. I can only vaguely remember it, but I remember this big screen behind her, and the number would come up on the big screen, and she would call it out. I think there was a lectern or a stand where she stood, and she let me have a go on the microphone and say, 'Good evening' to everyone. Of course, all the old dears were going, 'Ohh, how cute'. I would say [it was] before I started school.

A.F. It must have been smoky as well.

E.S. Yes, they would have been smoking in there, I remember. I had my birthday party at the Palace, and afterwards, we went into the Bingo hall just to give out party bags, and it still smelt quite smoky. I think it must have been my 12th or 13th. All of my friends and I met at the Kingsley Centre.

Then we got a pink limo from Kingsley to Alton, and we got there a little bit early, so the limo went down the high street, and it felt like everyone was looking at us. It was really cool. We booked the entire cinema out to see *St Trinians 2*. We sat there, and we had the whole cinema to ourselves. That felt really special, it felt like a film premiere sort of thing. It felt very grown up. I felt very cool, and then afterwards, we went into the bingo hall, where we gave out party bags. So we hired it out not thinking we'd fill it but it was just to give that feeling of fun. My family were friendly with Raj. I think he gave it to us a little bit cheaper. He's lovely. I think it was probably about ten, eleven, or twelve of us. Yes, it was lovely.

A.F. In the questionnaire, there is a question about shenanigans that kids get up to in the cinema and what they do. I wondered if there was any of that at your birthday party in terms of messing around and running about.

E.S. There probably was a little bit of messing around, but from the other kids. Whenever I went to the cinema, I was always really well-behaved, and I don't know if that's because my mum and my uncle worked there. I like to think so, anyway. I know some kids throw popcorn and stuff like that. I was more aware that someone would have to come and clean that up afterwards. But if I did misbehave, probably my biggest thing would be talking, whispering, 'What's going on? What's going to happen next?' I want to know what happened next.

A.F. So what are your thoughts on the Palace closing?

E.S. I think I was sad when I first heard about it. But then, actually, I thought, well, the last time I went was pre-pandemic. So if I went, it was only once every few years. So, it is sad but not surprising. In a way, the sadness comes from the fact that it's always been there. Driving past and seeing Raj standing outside in his suit, looking really smart. It's so strange, but things do change. You weren't just going to see a film. You were going to experience something, and you're going to make memories.

I suppose some of the sadness for me from the Palace closing is that it is a place that I associate with my mum, who isn't here anymore, and that's kind of sad, but like I said, not surprising. You can't really think of the Palace without thinking of Raj. I mean, to me, anyway, I don't know how long he's owned it.

A.F. I think he said it was twenty eight years. He said that when he bought it, the previous owner said, 'I'll give you three years before you close'. So he's done an amazing job for the town.

E.S. When you think of how many people he's given happy memories.

A.F. Yes. We've heard some great stories of people running late, calling him up, and asking, 'Can you hold the film? We'll be there in 15 minutes.' And him saying, 'OK, I'll stall a bit'.

E.S. Wow, yes, the Vue wouldn't do that for you, that's for sure –that real personal touch. It's an amazing project that you're doing to collect all these memories because a cinema or any sort of collective cultural space is such an important part of the story.

I think because, of course, the cinema, it's the building, it's projection, but it's also the people who inhabit it. Well, it's Raj for a start. He's the heart of it. But then he wouldn't have kept it going for twenty eight years if people hadn't been there. The cinema is the people watching and the people in it as much as the films [they're watching], and it tells the story of a town in many ways, I think. I think sometimes people don't even realize they remember things until they're asked; it's like you're being given those memories back in some ways, which is really nice.

I remember seeing *Spy Kids 3* and that was a 3D film. 3D was all new and really exciting at the time. Back then, it was the cardboard 3D glasses; one eye was blue, and one eye was red. Looking back now, if I were probably to go and watch that film in 3D again, I'd think, 'This is rubbish.' But at the time, I thought it was the most incredible thing.

A.F. You've given us a lot of really beautiful and vivid memories. Thank you.

WHAT ARE YOUR THOUGHTS ON WATCHING FILMS IN A CINEMA?

PREFER THE CINEMA - LARGE SCREEN.

Nice to go in a group and go to the Railway to discuss the film afterwards, we did this.

I GET EXCITED.

I LOVE FILMS.

HOW IS IT DIFFERENT TO WATCHING AT HOME DO YOU THINK?

WHICH DO YOU PREFER?

I love watching films at home, but going to the cinema is completely different, it's a wonderful experience and is great to get out and go to something easy and relaxing.

I LOVE GOING TO THE CINEMA AND SEEING THINGS ON A BIG SCREEN IN A COLLECTIVE WAY.

I love going to the cinema... no phone distracting me, sit back, relax and get taken on a journey, laugh, cry, wince and everything in between.

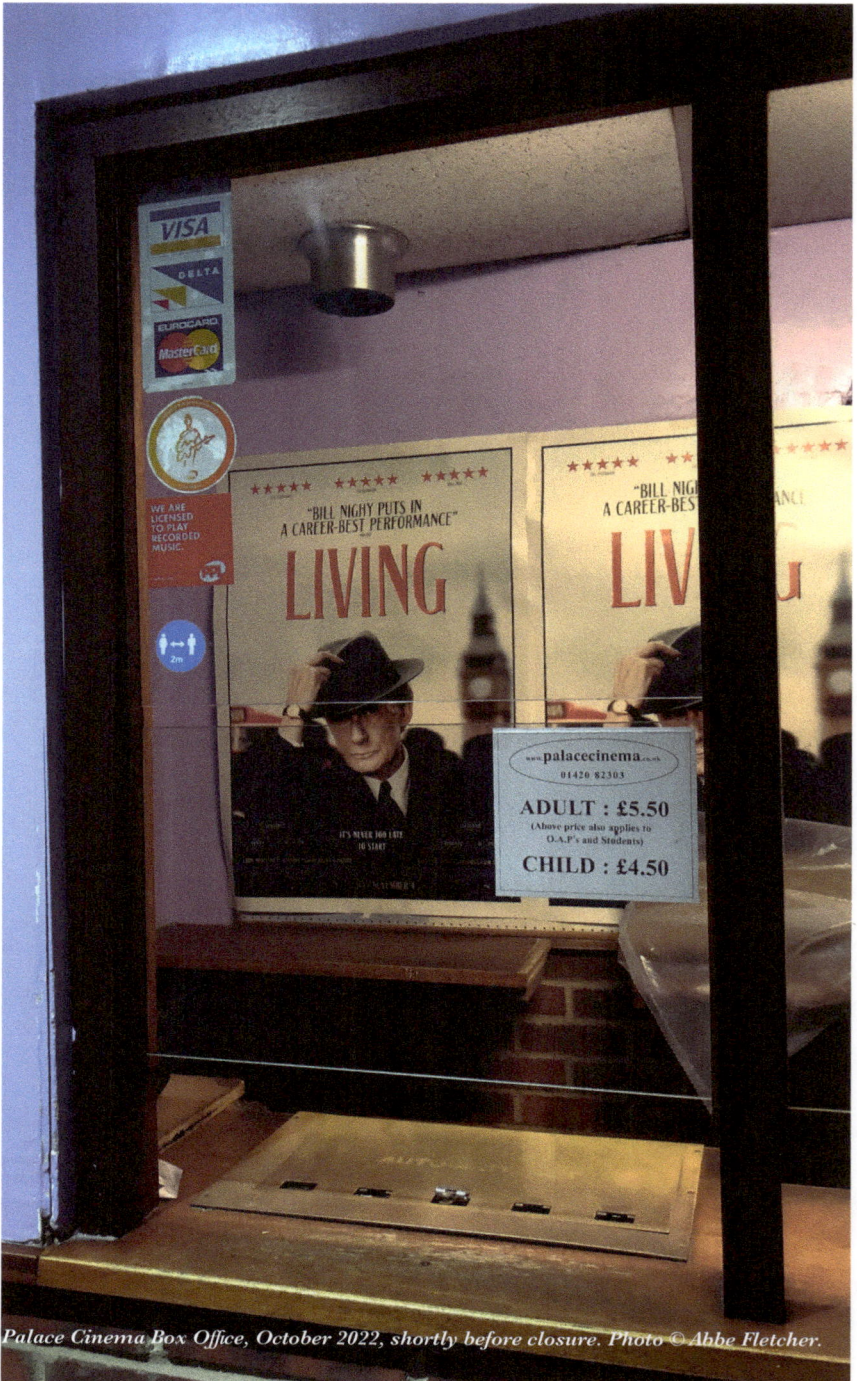

Palace Cinema Box Office, October 2022, shortly before closure. Photo © Abbe Fletcher.

Mandy O'Neill
Interviewed by Carol Palmer
19th November 2023

Carol Palmer: How do you know the Palace Cinema? Do you live in Alton?

Mandy O'Neill: Yes, I live in Alton and know the Palace Cinema as I was taken there by my mother as a child. We moved to Alton when I was five years old. It was a real big treat as money was tight. Mum would take us to see films of her choice, films like *The Black & White Minstrels*.

I remember that the screen showed loads of colourful bubbles all merging into one another, and this fascinated being only 5. This was just before the film came on. I remember the interval where the ice cream lady would come out. I do remember the little round tubs of vanilla ice cream and the tiny plastic spoon.

I thought the cinema was very exciting!

We went regularly when I was a child – usually every time a Disney film was on and when a musical that Mum liked was showing. Mum always liked the cinema and went often as a young person in Aldershot. She went to Saturday cinema and remembered the war newsreels that played first. So Mum really loved movies, especially musicals. As a teenager, I only saw *Grease*.

As an adult, I don't recall ever visiting Alton cinema, although I think I saw *Kramer Vs. Kramer.* I saw that film with Whitney Houston in *The Bodyguard.* Oh yes, and we saw *Herbie.*

C.P. And do you have any memories of any shenanigans from childhood cinema visits?

M.O. I remember the cinema being divided into two floors and there was just one auditorium with a balcony. As teens watching *Grease*, boys would chuck bits of food or rubbish at us. My friend was giggling so much that we were nearly thrown out!

C.P. Which films do you remember seeing at the Palace?

M.O. Mostly Disney, such as *Dumbo, Pinocchio, Snow White & the Seven Dwarfs, Bambi*. Also, *Chitty Chitty Bang Bang*, which I loved, apart from the Child Catcher!

A lot of the Disney films were scary, too. *Dumbo* has some bizarre scenes of elephants morphing into all kinds of evil-looking monsters! Also, we saw *Song of the South* and *The Sound of Music*.

C.P. I remember going to see *101 Dalmatians* with my first husband when I was expecting my first child. I hadn't seen that one as a child! So that was 1984 or 1985. So it was about 1970 to 1975 when we went quite regularly. The last film I saw at the cinema was *Grease*. That must have been around 1979. I had a major crush on John Travolta after that! I never went on my own. I went to the cinema with school friends; I think it was to see *Grease* again.

C.P. What refreshments would you usually take or buy there?

M.O. As a kid, sometimes mum bought us an ice cream. In later life, you bought your refreshments in the foyer, where you could buy popcorn, chocolate bars and cans of fizzy.

C.P. What are your thoughts on the closure of the Palace Cinema in Alton?

M.O. I think that it should have remained a cinema with all of its history on display in the foyer – a gallery if you like. The facade should have been restored to its original style.

'I THOUGHT THE CINEMA WAS VERY EXCITING! WE WENT REGULARLY WHEN I WAS A CHILD – USUALLY EVERY TIME A DISNEY FILM WAS ON...'

The Palace Cinema, 2001. Photo by © Tony Cross.

WHAT DO YOU REMEMBER ABOUT ALTON AS A YOUNG PERSON? WHAT ENTERTAINMENT WAS THERE OTHER THAN THE PALACE CINEMA?

AS A 17, 18, 19 YEAR OLD IT WAS NORMALLY THE PUB. DRIVING TO BASINGSTOKE CINEMA WAS ALSO COMMON AS THE MULTIPLEX WAS NEW.

I ONLY MOVED TO ALTON IN 2007, SO AS SOMEONE YOUNG AT HEART AT LEAST, I WAS PLEASED TO FIND A CINEMA THAT MY KIDS COULD GROW UP WITH CHARGING LESS THAN £5 PER TICKET. OTHER CINEMAS WERE A DRIVE AWAY AND, APART FROM A FEW FILMS SHOWN FOR A PERIOD AT THE WESSEX ARTS CENTRE AROUND 2013-2014, MUCH MORE EXPENSIVE.

You could either go to the sports centre or the cinema…and the community centre held discos.

Most people knew each other. Not many places to go apart from pubs.

Nothing, the cinema was the best bit about it.

Disco also held at the cinema and the assembly rooms.

NOT MUCH BOYS CLUB AND PUBS DIDN'T OPEN UNTIL 7PM ON SUNDAYS.

I REMEMBER DISCOS AT THE WHITE HORSE AND THE CATHOLIC CHURCH AND GOING ON PUB CRAWLS AROUND THE TOWN FROM THE YOUNG AGE OF ABOUT 14.

The Allen gallery-upstairs where you could do colouring. The park.

Dancing in a cellar club in Turk Street.

A DANCE STUDIO BY THE NEW SAINSBURY'S, THE PARK AND THE COMMUNITY CENTRE DISCO.

SMALL TOWN, LIMITED THINGS TO DO. SPORTS CENTRE WAS A KEY FOCAL POINT.

DANCES IN THE ASSEMBLY ROOMS, RENDEZVOUS CAFE BAR WITH PINBALL MACHINES.

If we went to watch a film we always wanted to sit upstairs on the balcony that was the best bit. When I was about 16 they started doing discos I think they were on a Wednesday night. All my friends used to go for a dance. I also worked here at the bingo sessions as a teenager. I sold the tickets and then when someone shouted for bingo I checked off the numbers. At the half time break I sold teas and coffees and CUPaSOUPS. I also occasionally worked the cloak room at the discos.

The view of the box office from inside the cinema doors, 2022. Photo © Abbe Fletcher

Palace Cinema seating in Screen 1. Taken on the final day the Palace was open, 30th October 2022.
Photo © Abbe Fletcher

Geraldine Dawson
Interview by Abbe Fletcher
14th July 2023

Geraldine Dawson: We moved to Alton in 1993, having moved down from Farnham. Cinema was one of the reasons to move, one of my new neighbours was a keen cinema fan. She introduced me to Raj.

Abbe Fletcher: Do you remember your first trip?

G.D. Maybe, it was *Il Postino*, which I do believe is one of Raj's favourite films. I remember seeing *Romeo and Juliet* there. We used to go to the cinema a lot – often to Basingstoke, sometimes to London and regularly to the Palace. The advantage of the Palace was that it was easy to go midweek. Once we'd had children, we probably saw more films in Alton – time and money allowing. It was great to be a five minute walk from the cinema. You'd just phone Raj and say, 'It's me. Can I have two tickets?' Then he would say, 'Well, it's not going to be busy so don't worry,' or 'It is busy, where do you want to sit?' It was that easy! It was easy to get to know Raj because he was in Alton every day, often standing on 'the stoop' and he was always keen to talk. Once I knew him a little better, I felt able to put in requests for films. Especially those films that were not likely to be shown at Vue or Odeon – more independent and foreign language films. More often than not he would screen the film.

He was responsive. He did have really good film knowledge. Whatever the film he would always be aware of it – what it was about and how it was being received.

The joy was that the programme that Raj offered was a mix of the popular: James Bond, anything Jane Austen or Judy Dench. I think Colin Farrell was particularly popular with the Alton audience. And the unusual, the less popular, and even though some screenings would have had only a few customers, he continued to offer that variety. It was such a treat to have access to a variety of films while living out in the sticks!

Once I knew him better, I began to ask why he was using the downstairs space for bingo rather than cinema – he was clear that for those who loved bingo, he would continue to offer it, as long as there was a demand. I think in the 1990s he had quite a few users. And the cinema was really affordable. You know when you've got young children, you're paying for everything, and paying a mortgage, and it's really important to have access to affordable and fun leisure activities.

'I CALLED RAJ, TOLD HIM WHERE I WAS AND ASKED HIM IF HE COULD DELAY THE FILM...'

A.F. You had a rather lovely story that I always remember. Could you tell the story?

G.D. Oh yes it was a Roddy Doyle film, *Millions* about catholic brothers whose mother has died and the youngest boy accidentally comes across a hoard of stolen cash – lovely film! It was a Sunday matinee, 3pm start. I decided to go to Winchester beforehand with the children and a friend. Stupidly, I forgot the time and we were only leaving Winchester just before 3pm. Since I didn't want to spoil the film for the children I called Raj, told him where I was and asked him if he could delay the film until 3.15 pm. He told me to be there by 3.15 pm. We made it just in time. I deposited the children and friend, luckily found a parking space and sat down just as the film was starting. Where else would you get that kind of service?

The children still remember that film fondly. Children were able to go to the cinema, without their parents, when they were very young. I mean, if it had been an evening film, he couldn't have done it, but it was a matinee.

A.F. I love it.

G.D. There was a group of us that used to run and take part regularly in sponsored events. We had decided to take part in the

Clarendon Way walk – between Winchester and Salisbury – for Naomi House Children's Hospice.

Although keen to do the event, we were all struggling to know just how we would raise the required sponsorship monies. None of us wanted to ask friends, family or work colleagues for any more sponsorship money, they were all sponsored out! I suggested that we hire the cinema and show a film, make it an event and give the profits to the charity. The key was getting a crowd-pleasing film. I looked at the upcoming films and had heard good things about *Slumdog Millionaire*. I approached Raj and asked if we could have his first night for this film. He was happy with this and we paid him £500 for the large screen. The tickets sold quickly to friends and family. I think we charged £12 for a ticket, drink and some canapés. We sold 110 tickets, sold ice cream at the interval and held a raffle. I don't remember the actual number, but we raised just under £1000 for Naomi House. And the film was great!

A.F. That's a great story.

G.D. He always said he'd be happy to [hire out the screen]. He said, 'You could have the first night of James Bond if you want.' I don't think it was uncommon for people to hire the screen for a big event.

A.F. Did you take your children to see children's films there, or did you just take them with you?

G.D. We did when they were small. I remember two of the worst films I think I've ever seen: *Scooby Doo* and *Star Wars: Revenge of the Sith*. The only consolation was that tickets weren't expensive!

'I DO TRY TO SEE FILMS FOR THE FIRST TIME ON THE BIG SCREEN...'

A.F. How regularly would you go?

G.D. I think Autumn and Spring were the most popular time for films.

'...NOW THAT THE PALACE IS CLOSED IT IS MORE DIFFICULT TO SEE THEM FOR A SECOND TIME ON A BIG SCREEN.'

Raj was good at getting a great range of films, so I probably went quite regularly. What was great about the Palace was that I felt able to see films for a second or even a third time! I saw the French film *[The] Intouchables* at Winchester Everyman. I loved it and told my friends about it, so when Raj screened it, I went along with them to see it again. Also, *Little Miss Sunshine* – again, I saw it, maybe at Basingstoke and told my friends about it, they liked it so much we watched it twice at the Palace! This kind of indulgence was only possible because the cinema was on our doorstep and it was affordable.

I do try to see films for the first time on the big screen. Now that the Palace is closed it is more difficult to see them for a second time on a big screen. I will watch films again at home and of course TVs are bigger than they used to be, but still, it is not the same. I don't believe that a film such as *The Assassination of Jesse James by the Coward Robert Ford* can be watched and appreciated on a TV. The cinematography, the sound, the scale of the setting is so beautiful and cannot be captured on a small screen. There are too many distractions at home.

A.F. It won't hold your attention. It's just such a different [experience].

G.D. It's an art form.

A.F. An art form that you experience with other people. I like the message they have at the beginning of cinema screenings about putting your phones away and giving over to this experience. Everything's interruptible now.

G.D. You get lost in it.

A.F. Yes, even more so since lockdown, I think.

G.D. I was still feeling nervous, not to mention scared, about mixing in public [when lockdown was lifted]. But we decided to see *Tenet*. I booked a morning screening, hoping it would be quieter, and it was. The cinemas were insisting on spaces between parties and mask wearing throughout.

We saw the film at Vue Portsmouth on a huge screen, with brilliant sound and I loved it. The whole experience was quite overwhelming and wonderful. Cinema was, for a time, back in our lives. My worries about Covid didn't abate, but I took care to pick and choose times I thought would be less busy. I felt this pull of wanting to be in the cinema but needing to keep safe.

We often hear that younger people don't want to watch big screen films but I don't agree with that. If they have access to a cinema, they will go. Alton has a range of film and media studies courses – this is a group of young people who would be regular users, if not contributors, to a local cinema. Also, a local cinema means that they don't have to rely on others to taxi them about! There is no reason why they wouldn't want to experience a film on the big screen.

A.F. It used to be such a mass medium that people would go and see whatever was on. That's what was great about the Palace, you'd have the latest release and you have the option of just going to see what was just coming out in London or anywhere across the country, that same night.

G.D. That's where the Palace was so brilliant: we could see the blockbusters or the quirky. It can be frustrating to read film reviews about new releases and know that they won't be screened near you.

A.F. It's great to hear you talk about cinema as a medium to be experienced in big scale, in the dark, with the sound and with other people in there.

G.D. With that, it's projected the way it's meant to be projected. You are getting [the creation] the cinematographer and the director and all the actors [had] in their minds.

A.F. Yes, absolutely. Also, that idea of stories and we need stories.

G.D. Communal experience and how we make sense of our lives. In this idea of identifying with the story, identifying with the character and their journey and just forgetting about the outside world.

A.F. Exactly. Rather than it being something that is for the elite or exclusive. We screened *Brief Encounter* at the Allen Gallery little pop-up cinema. An old classic black and white British film.

G.D. How many people have seen it on a big screen?

A.F. We sold out days before the screening. We purposely put this on. Definitely wanted to show something classic. People in the feedback had wanted classic black and white.

Watching it with people who were familiar with it but probably haven't seen it for decades and haven't seen it on the big screen or since the time. There was this feeling in the room, the emotion of that film.

G.D. We used to have Friday night as film night, and I would buy DVDs of all the films I loved when I was growing up and that don't seem to be on TV anymore. For example, *Barefoot in the Park, In the Heat of the Night, Bringing Up Baby*!

The other thing I remember was when the children were at Anstey Junior the year 6 children were taken to the cinema (I think it was a summer term treat) to see a film. For some of the children it was the first time they had been to the cinema! I don't remember the films they saw, but they would have had a link to their studies.

A.F. I think St Lawrence also used to take children to the cinema. What are your thoughts on the closing of the Palace?

G.D. I'm quite bereft that there isn't a cinema. I still hold out hope that we can have a screen [in Alton]. I think it's a great loss to the community – but I do believe that if a new cinema was opened, people of all ages would use it. It would just be such a joy for so many people in the town. It's the convenience. It's about not having to jump in your car or get on the train or spend extra money. Like we've said, it's about walking to something that can fill you with all kinds of emotions and it's there, and I think it could be there again.

What you're doing with pop up cinema at the [Allen] Gallery, that's great because it keeps people interested. I think Alton needs a cinema.

A.F. That's the phrase that captures so much I think – to have affordable entertainment in the town.

G.D. They have ownership of it, it becomes theirs and that's when people start using it because you do those things where you have a birthday party or you think, 'Can I book the screen for this special event?' People then take ownership of it. It's been there before and we have to keep faith that it can be there again, this just is a blip I think. It's always been my dream to have a cinema.

> 'YOU [HAD] THE OPTION OF...GOING TO SEE WHAT WAS JUST COMING OUT IN LONDON OR ANYWHERE ACROSS THE COUNTRY, THAT SAME NIGHT.'

A.F. Well, I likewise always wanted to program films, and wherever I've been as a lecturer and a student I'd always put screenings on. Nancy introduced me on Saturday nights saying, 'Abbe, is – well she's our programmer.'

When we were thinking about how we could save the cinema, I had dreams about running one. I think in terms of meeting people. This is what's been so wonderful about the Save the Cinema group and about the Memories of the Palace and the Allen Gallery and getting to know people in the town through a love of cinema and finding other cinephiles has been so inspiring to me.

G.D. They're out there.

A.F. We're doing what we can do now but I think if we keep this idea and this love of cinema – or record the fact that there was a cinema in the town – going between a range of people, you've more chance of spotting the opportunity.

G.D. Yes, between us.

A.F. This idea of cinema as a medium and that people also love it.

G.D. It's not just my generation or your generation, it's my son's generation and I'm sure children coming through whose parents are still taking them to the cinema want that experience on the big screen.

A.F. It can't just disappear like that.

> 'WHEN WE WERE THINKING ABOUT HOW WE COULD SAVE THE CINEMA, I HAD DREAMS ABOUT RUNNING ONE. I THINK IN TERMS OF MEETING PEOPLE.'

Final curtain falls for Palace Cinema

BY PAUL COATES
paul.coates@farnhamherald.com
07508 848327

THE PALACE CINEMA in Alton has finally closed after 110 years – 85 of them in the current Art Deco building which is up for sale at £850,000.

Raj Jeyasingam, who owned the independent cinema in Normandy Street for its last 27 years, announced in July 2021 that he would shut it in September 2022 if nobody could meet his asking price.

A second sign for the Hampshire Lettings Company next door has now signalled the end by replacing the Palace Cinema sign over the picture house doors.

Members of the Save Alton Cinema campaign admit there is "little prospect" of any more films being shown in the building designed by architect Robin A Thomas and opened with *Poor Little Rich Girl* starring Shirley Temple. But they are searching for ways to retain the cinema experience in the town while preserving memories of the Palace.

The white Hampshire Lettings Company sign is over the cinema door

Campaigner Tim Woolman said: "We're very sad to have lost the Palace Cinema, but we remain hopeful about the future. Almost 3,000 people cared enough to sign our petition, and more than 300 filled out a survey sharing their views, showing there is a good appetite for cinema-going, given a suitable combination of experience, location and price.

"The Save Alton Cinema campaign has searched for alternative venues suited to showing films, working with people who have some knowledge of suitable rooms and licensing to cover the venue and the copyright for the public screening.

"Four venues have expressed interest in showing films, at least occasionally, so if and when that happens we will support them as much as possible.

"In the background, ambitions continue for a more cinema-like facility in the town.

"However, bringing together the funding, venue and team resources will need a lot of support. We welcome people's suggestions via email to save altoncinema@gmail.com"

The Memories of The Palace Cinema Alton project team is compiling an oral history of cinema-going in Alton to be stored at the Curtis Museum.

So far memories have included Saturday kids' clubs, sold-out showings of *The Full Monty* and discos in the 1970s.

Project lead Abbe Fletcher said: "It's wonderful to hear what an impact the cinema has had on people's lives."

The next Record Your Memories event will be held at Alton Community Centre on November 19 from 2pm to 4pm.

The Palace Cinema closes for the final time. Alton Herald, 10th November 2022.

Film fans may buy cinema

By Moira Howells

AN innovative way to mobilise the 'Big Society' into ensuring that Alton continues to support its own cinema, is receiving an enthusiastic airing over the internet.

The idea, floated by local resident, Penney Hames, is to start a co-operative, with the aim of raising enough money to buy the Palace Cinema and to refurbish and run it for posterity.

Palace Cinema owner Raj Jeyasingam believes it is an idea that could succeed.

He has a dilemma in that while the bingo hall, that takes up part of the building, has a loyal and enthusiastic following, numbers are falling.

The rising popularity of online bingo offering big money prizes means that young people in particular are turning their backs on conventional bingo halls.

In the past bingo has supported the two screen cinema, along with a flat and an adjoining shop, that both bring in rent.

But, with bingo on the decline, and despite his wish to continue supporting those in the community who enjoy playing at the Palace, Mr Jeyasingam is having to take stock of his position.

A businessman with "a passion for film" who has always regarded his ownership of the Palace as "a paid hobby", the time is fast approaching when it will require further investment.

The advance in digital technology is bringing pressure to introduce digital projectors at a cost of around £80,000 each and, he says, the seats in the upper studio need replacing.

Mr Jeyasingam has sought to tighten his belt by taking on the role of manager himself but this brings additional pressure if, for any reason, he is unable to get to Alton from his London home, to open up. And there will come a time when he wants to retire.

His solution, at present, is to seek planning permission to redevelop the bingo hall into seven flats – six two bedroom with a studio flat above, on three levels and with underground parking for six cars. Access would be via the service road at the rear of the property.

If granted, the money from this initiative would enable him to reinvest in the cinema.

"But," he told the Herald, "it is not about the money anymore. I am in a position to shut up shop and walk away if I have to, but I want to do my best to leave the town with a cinema."

While the building is not listed and could be ripe for development, Mr Jeyasingam would rather see it continue in its current role.

He is looking for a figure of £1.3 million for the freehold of the entire site, but would be willing, if granted permission to build the flats, to release the rest of the building for a figure in the region of £800,000.

He believes there is scope within the cinema to introduce a wine bar and to upgrade the screen areas. And, he feels, there is enough customer support within Alton and the surrounding area, to be able to make a go of it.

Having talked to Mr Jeyasingam about the future of the cinema, and being interested in co-operative working in relation to the Alton Food Initiative's Community Farm, of which she is a driving force, Mrs Hames decided to do some digging.

She discovered that campaigners in Cumbria were seeking to save a 100-year-old cinema in Penrith by staging a co-operative take-over. Thousands of cinemagoers are asked to invest £150 each to enable the Lonsdale Alhambra cinema to be run by a co-operative.

The determination and ingenuity of the people of Penrith to save their local cinema strengthened Mrs Hames' decision to "start the ball rolling" over a similar scheme in Alton.

Having sought reassurance from Mr Jeyasingam that he would "love a community group to buy the cinema", she has sought to float the idea by sending an e-mail that has found its way into many people's inboxes.

She says: "I think our local cinema has seen better days but I love going there just because it is local and I know that a lot of other people do as well. I think that it's a wonderful resource for a small town like ours and it would be a great shame if it closed."

While Mrs Hames admits to having no experience of starting a co-operative she has checked with Co-operatives UK who, she says, would provide useful information and support.

She understands that on top of the purchase price money would have to be found to refurbish the cinema, but she believes there are people within the local community who have the skills to help.

She said: "I imagine that this sort of project will need architects, marketing people, electricians, accountants, local politicians, carpenters, fundraisers, solicitors, webdesigners, plumbers, printers, administrators, typists, organisers and a whole host of other people who just love the idea of local cinema."

If there is sufficient interest shown the aim will be to schedule a meeting to think about the next step in staging a possible co-operative buy-out of the Palace Cinema.

For further information contact Penney Hames on 07811 217744.

DID YOU GO TO THE

BINGO

OR

WRESTLING

OR ANY OTHER EVENTS

AT THE

PALACE

CINEMA?

WHAT WERE THEY LIKE?

No but did go to live screenings

of *Yerma*, *Hamlet*, Opera, ballet .

MY AUNT USED
TO LOVE THE
WRESTLING
THERE IN THE
1970S.

WENT TO DISCOS ON
WEDNESDAYS. THEY
WERE GOOD AND BUSY.

PALACE VICTIM OF THE VIDEO AGE

ALTON'S Palace Cinema shows its last film tonight (Wednesday), ending a 70 year tradition in the town.

With attendances falling and the home video market booming, the decision to close the cinema was, perhaps, inevitable.

"Our audiences have dropped by 50 per cent since this time last year," said Mr. Nigel Moyce, manager of the Palace, which first opened its doors in 1914.

"We just cannot compete with the video industry. You can hire a film for the whole family to enjoy for about £1 but we have to ask around £2 a head," he said.

However, the bingo sessions and discos at the Palace are to continue and it is hoped that one day the projectors could be back in action.

"The cinema industry has gone through bad times before but has recovered," said Mr. Moyce.

"We are keeping the facility for showing films, and maybe, if things improve, we can open up again," he said.

There is also a possibility that special afternoon matinees will be arranged for school holiday periods.

The Palace is the second cinema to be closed down by owners, Spedeworth International, who, earlier this year, shut down Bordon's picture house.

But their one remaining cinema, the Savoy at Petersfield, is safe, at least for the time being.

"If things continue as they are we can keep the Savoy open but these are sad times for the industry," said Mr. Moyce.

The cinema tradition that began in Alton with great names like Chaplin, Keaton and Gish ends in somewhat less style with "The Party Animal."

It is all a far cry from the Palace's hey-day when as Alton historian Mr. Charles Hawkins records: "Saturday nights brought long queues and patrons paid to stand around the walls if seats weren't available."

In the 1930's, a petition was signed by patrons calling for the cinema to open on Sundays and it enjoyed full houses throughout and after the war.

Bingo was introduced when television began to make serious inroads into the film audience.

Mr. Raymond Porter of Porter's Video Centre agreed that, following an initial boom, the video industry had settled down to "healthy" and steady expansion.

He also said: "It is very sad to see a cinema go but I don't think it is wholly the fault of video.

"The sad fact is that rural cinemas have been closing down in ever increasing numbers for many years," he said.

—The all-new cinema re-opens on Boxing Day

ALTON is to have its cinema back. The Palace in Normandy Street will be back in business on Boxing Day with an entirely new look.

Refurbishment of the cinema gallery, which began in September, has now resulted in the provision of a 111-seat luxury studio with blue decor and the latest in projection equipment.

The aim is to provide the best in comfort, light and sound.

In the past, the Palace has boasted "one of the biggest cinema screens in the south, but it didn't have the quality of sound and light," said proprietor Mark Eaton.

Nevertheless, at a total cost of £40,000 the new studio boasts a fine 16-feet screen "which, for a studio of this size, is quite big", a new tower projection system, a Xenon lamp to replace the old carbon arch light system for a more powerful and constant light, and a new amplification system, with stereo processors and four channel amplifiers to feed seven auditorium speakers, which should give the very best in sound.

Within the studio, the balcony has been re-terraced to provide more leg room and a way for comfortable modern seating, while convector heating replaces the old heating system to provide extra comfort.

The studio with its wall-to-wall carpeting and spacious new stage would make an attractive conference room, said Mr. Eaton.

The decision to revamp the cinema was a difficult one to make. Mr. Eaton had tried showing films three days a week on the evening when there were bingo sessions. But the cinema side wasn't paying.

"It was a case of do or die. Either we had to show films a night a week or close the cinema," added Mr. Eaton.

In the event, he decided to take a chance and convert the gallery area into a studio, leaving the already refurbished ground floor to the popular Bingo and Social Club.

The Delinquents

The cinema will re-open with showing to coincide with the West End release of The Delinquents starring Kylie Minogue and Charlie Schlatter.

The film will run for 10 days, to be followed, on January 6th, seven days of Indiana Jones and the Last Crusade.

"During our closure, the Palace has missed out on a lot of good films which we feel need showing. During the next few months, it is our aim to show a host of box office greats along with current releases," said Mr. Eaton.

Also in January cinema-goers can expect to see Back to the Future II, Ghostbusters II and Disney's Oliver and Company.

Bingo will continue as usual, with the cinema studio open seven days a week, showing evening performances daily and matinees during school holidays. An advanced booking service will also be available on Alton 82305 to overcome the problem of queueing.

Mr. Eaton is firmly convinced that it is the "quality that counts" and feels that the new Palace studio cinema will provide the right mix of decor, production and comfort for an enjoyable evening out, at a reasonable price.

And next year's project? "It is to smarten up the front of the building," said Mr. Eaton.

New owner for cinema

ALTON'S Palace Cinema is under new ownership and there are plans to show films seven nights a week.

Twenty-nine-year-old Mark Eaton has bought the premises from his father who owns Spedeworth Ltd., the stock car and greyhound racing circuit at Tongham, near Aldershot.

Mr. Eaton, who lives at Bishops Sutton but intends to move to Alton, says that the changes will not take place immediately and will not affect the regular bingo games.

"In around nine months time I intend spending some money on the place and hope to put in a second floor. Then we can run the cinema every night of the week as well as some other activities.

"At the moment with the cinema being purpose-built we can only run one function at a time. Bingo takes preference because obviously it is a bigger money spinner. But I think if we had a small film studio it should work very well."

One reason behind the move is the fact that distributors refuse to release current hit movies to outlets which screen them only a few times a week. "By the time they get to Alton everyone's seen them elsewhere," said the new owner.

Asked if the proposition was viable given the closure of cinemas up and down the country, Mr. Eaton said: "There is a problem in larger towns but in small places like Alton the youngsters really have nothing else to do, so it should work".

The first change happens later this month when there will be late Friday and Saturday night screenings starting at 10 p.m. The move coincides with the coming of the huge box office success Fatal Attraction.

The former manager Nigel Moyce completed his last night at the Palace on Saturday. After 15 years in the business he has decided "its time to make a break and broaden my horizons."

He is going to work for a catering supply company in Farnham.

"I've made a lot of friends and enjoyed my time here. It's always a pleasure to see..."

Plush at the Palace

Alton's Palace Cinema re-opens its completely refurbished 111-seat luxury studio on Boxing Day.

The conversion includes new projection equipment running on one projector with the latest tower run-off system and a more powerful trouble-free light source.

A completely new amplification system includes stereo processors and seven auditorium speakers to give the very best in sound.

Within the studio, the old balcony has been re-terraced to give more leg room and make way for the very latest design in cinema seating.

Complete new convector heating replaces the old system to add to the comfort.

The cinema will be open seven days a week with two performances daily and matinee performances during school holiday periods. An advanced booking service is on Alton (0420) 82305.

During closure, the Palace has missed out on a lot of good films and, during the next few months, it is the aim to show these "box office greats" along with current releases.

The Boxing Day re-opening coincides with the West End release of "The Delinquents," starring Kylie Minogue and Charlie Schlatter, showing for ten days.

The next few weeks at the Palace look something like this: January 6th—"Indiana Jones and the Last Crusade" (7 days); January 12th — "Back to the Future II," (14 days); January 26th — "Ghostbusters II." (14 days); February 9th—"Oliver and Company" (14 days).

20 Dec. 1989

Alton & Hampshire Herald cuttings, © *Curtis Museum*

Tim Woolman
Interview by Chris Stone
4th November 2023

Chris Stone: How was it that you know the Palace Cinema?

Tim Woolman: When we moved to Alton back in 2007, I was delighted to see that there was a cinema just a five-minute walk from where we were moving to. With young children, we were looking to be somewhere where we could walk with them, and when they grew up, they could go to places like the cinema themselves.

I can remember going to the cinema in the town I grew up. That was part of my childhood. Every generation finds its own films to grow up with, so it was great for them to look forward to that in Alton.

C.S. Can you remember the first film you saw at the Palace Cinema?

T.W. I am not sure I can remember the first film. We know what it is like to have to budget fairly carefully for family activities, so the low ticket prices at the Palace Cinema were really helpful, and we looked forward to a school holiday treat in particular.

C.S. What do you remember about the Cinema at that time?

T.W. I remember there was certainly a difference between going to the Palace Cinema and going to a multiplex. The tickets were cheaper. I like the fact that you could have a chat with the person running the cinema, and you might bump into somebody you know in the town, because it's the local cinema that people go to, so it feels friendly.

C.S. How frequently did you manage to get to the cinema, and was it mainly family that you went with?

T.W. Yes. So, as the kids grew older, we would go to the Palace for a James Bond film, or more recently, I would invite some friends to come and see a film like *Dune*. Films like *Star Wars* and *Blade Runner* really benefit from being close to a big screen.

C.S. Are there any particular films you remember seeing at the Palace?

T.W. I remember seeing *Warhorse* about 2011, the kind of film where you want to chat with people afterwards, as they've just shared the same experience. That stuck in my mind.

Then things like the live streams from a London venue are slightly different. I remember the stage version of *Billy Elliot* and seeing *The Nutcracker* ballet, for example. The close-up views of the performers at those kinds of live streams certainly help you enjoy the performance; you can see the facial expressions as well. And it has a special live feel, especially when you have an interval, and then you feel you want to join in the applause at the end.

'YOU MIGHT BUMP INTO SOMEBODY YOU KNOW IN THE TOWN, BECAUSE IT'S THE LOCAL CINEMA THAT PEOPLE GO TO, SO IT FEELS FRIENDLY.'

C.S. So going to the cinema, it's very difficult to watch a film without having some sort of refreshment. So what was it that you used to take?

T.W. Yes, we would sometimes pop our own popcorn in advance to take.

C.S. I know there was bingo or wrestling at the Palace Cinema as well. Did you go and see any of those?

T.W. I didn't actually go in, but I did peek through the doors once to see the bar and seating area, and I think that was also used also for children's parties at the back before it was converted into flats.

Once you have seen the back area, it is certainly easier to imagine how the two screens used to be one big auditorium; the second screen upstairs was the balcony. I have heard people say they went to the wrestling when it was one big auditorium, so there's an incredible history from the days when the cinema was a real social hub for a variety of events for people in the community.

C.S. Have you been able to get to the cinema just before it closed?

T.W. Yes, hearing that it was due to close, I invited some friends to come and see *See How They Run*, which was based on Agatha Christie's *The Mousetrap*. So it was fun to go to the cinema just one last time in Alton.

C.S. There are lots of streaming sites where you could watch a film in the comfort of your armchair, but what is it about going to the cinema that makes it that little bit special?

T.W. It is an interesting thought. There's something about sitting in an auditorium. You've got the bigger screen; you've got a feeling of a kind of spectacle. The sound is often so much stronger and with great effects going on around you. It's partly, of course, a way to get together in a shared social space; it feels like an occasion. There are certain big-screen films that really need that extra special kind of magic that going to the cinema brings. So, it's a bit of a treat, and it's a great shame that the Palace has closed, so we'll have to see what else we can do.

C.S. That brings us on to other options to watch films in and around Alton. What are your thoughts on the closure of the Palace Cinema?

T.W. Well, it's sad. It's a building with a rich history, and I think that type of building could offer really good entertainment in a growing town such as Alton.

When the Palace Cinema was first up for sale, I signed up to help with the Alton Independent Cinema Project back in 2012.

With various others interested in seeing what could be done in and around Alton, we formed a little group called Experience Film. That ran for five years. We showed some films at Wessex Arts Centre in Alton College. We used to show films around Regency Week, so I remember the Jane Austen's stories like *Persuasion* and *Mansfield Park*. Later, we showed films at Frensham Heights School, which was a lovely venue; the Aldridge Theatre there welcomed us. So that was really good. We offered an experience with the film; so a jazz band with the film *Some Like It Hot*, we had a magician with a film called *The Prestige*, we had Scalextric between the films *Senna* and *Rush* – we had a double bill. We even showed *2001: A Space Odyssey* in the Winchester Planetarium. And live accompaniment to a triple bill of silent films. There are so many good things Experience Film did.

'THERE'S AN INCREDIBLE HISTORY FROM THE DAYS WHEN THE CINEMA WAS A REAL SOCIAL HUB FOR A VARIETY OF EVENTS FOR PEOPLE IN THE COMMUNITY.'

Then, when the Palace was more recently up for sale, seeing the respones to the Save Alton Cinema campaign, I think there's really a great interest in local entertainment offering a good experience. And I hope that includes films which aren't too expensive for families. The community centre has been trying that kind of thing.

Looking at community cinema options, the one in Fleet works really well. People come together at the Harlington Centre every couple of weeks, and there's a real buzz around a wide range of film screenings there. So I think that shows what works. I think they have hit a great formula. The friendly hosts there are keen to see what the audience appreciates. So, I find that a great inspiration.

I'm on the lookout for a suitable venue to help arrange more films in Alton. We are currently working with the Allen Gallery to show films monthly [Screen at the Allen Gallery in collaboration with the Memories of the Palace Cinema Oral History Project]. Although the gallery space is relatively small, we have a great evening.

It would be good to think about what we learn from trying to keep film showings alive; now that the Palace has closed, we can find a number of places where audiences will find what they would like to see.

I'm looking forward to the Alton Arts Festival in July [2024]. We'll see how we can integrate films with that.

The more you talk to people, the more you find there are various interests and possibilities. So, it's nice to be able to share what we can do with people and just reflect on the memories we've had and, hopefully, what we can look forward to.

C.S. Many thanks, Tim, for taking the time to have a chat about your memories of the Palace Cinema.

'IT'S NICE TO BE ABLE TO SHARE WHAT WE CAN DO WITH PEOPLE AND JUST REFLECT ON THE MEMORIES WE'VE HAD AND, HOPEFULLY, WHAT WE CAN LOOK FORWARD TO.'

DO YOU THINK
YOU WOULD GO
TO THE CINEMA
IN ALTON IF
IT WERE IN
A DIFFERENT
VENUE THAN THE
PALACE?

YES

Yes if we can walk there !

Definitely. Nothing beats it. Soon it will be the only place where you can't be distracted by a mobile phone!

Yes, definitely, assuming the price and programming is right.

Yes. A shame it seems there is no future in the Palace cinema, but I'd still go to a different Alton cinema venue.

Yes. But I don't think it would be financially viable. People won't use it enough

If it was independent

Possibly not. I love the character of the building and the original fixtures. Going to a modern cinema is like watching a film at home...there is nothing unique about a vue or an odeon

NO

WILL YOU TRAVEL
TO FARNHAM,
LIPHOOK OR
BASINGSTOKE
TO GO TO THE
CINEMA NOW
THE PALACE IS
CLOSED?

Basingstoke
Odeon

Basingstoke
Vue

I live in London
but when I go back
to Hampshire we
go to Farnham
or Winchester for
cinema

YES

Go to Port
Solent

Reluctantly, but
I love Marvel
too much to stop
going altogether

I already
do this

NO

I'm not sure I
will bother with
movie watching
if I have to
travel.

Pip Eldridge
Interviewed by Chris Stone
4th November 2023

Chris Stone: Do you remember your first visit to the Cinema?

Pip Eldridge: I do. I actually texted my mum and I said, 'Do you remember the first time that you took us here?' because I grew up in Holybourne, born in 1972, and I don't know exactly when it was, but my mum brought my younger sister and I to come and see *Bambi*. It was when the cinema still had a balcony and it felt very large. It was a much more beautiful and impressive space at that point. I remember, clearly, it's really traumatizing that film. I don't know why they send small children to go and see films like *Bambi* because the beginning is absolutely harrowing.

I remember this little girl on the left side of my mum, bent over to my mum and went, 'Oi, are you crying?' and my mum went, 'Oh, yes, I am crying'. But that was the first time. I think we went to see a lot of Disney films, I remember seeing *Dumbo* there, *Bedknobs and Broomsticks* there. And I was thinking about the later stages because I moved out of Holybourne, or Alton when I was 18 to go to university, but I do remember seeing *Ghostbusters*; that was a really big thing. And I remember seeing *Rain Man* there as well. And later, because we moved back to just outside Alton in 2012 when my kids were quite little, we came to see *Shaun the Sheep*. There's a lot of jeopardy in *Shaun the Sheep* for small children and my daughter got up and actually ran out of the cinema. So, we all had to leave because she was too scared.

C.S. So, going to see those films, was it predominantly family that you went with?

P.E. I think that when I went to see *Rain Man*, I think that was with a group of friends, and we were dropped off. Quite often, we were driven and dropped off by the church so we could cross the road and walk in.

'I REMEMBER *MARY POPPINS* VERY WELL, AND BEING AT THE CINEMA WAS REALLY, REALLY EXCITING...'

Actually, most of my early memories it is going to see the children's films that were there.

C.S. Are there any particular film stars or films, that hold a special memory for you?

P.E. Film stars, well, funnily enough, not from the Palace. Actually, I can pinpoint whenever I saw a particular type of film and where I was because we went to see films in Guildford quite often and also down in Winchester. The ones I saw at the cinema, that I can really remember because you didn't go to the cinema so much at that time when you were that age. So I remember *Mary Poppins* very well, and being at the cinema was really, really exciting. I remember seeing *Top Gun* in Guildford and my Dad sneaking my friend and me in because we were a year too young; because I think it was a 15 certificate. And then I returned the favour to him when *Top Gun* came out recently, I took him. So we went, just the two of us; it was really nice, actually. Major stars? I guess I always loved the films, but I wasn't so star-orientated.

C.S. I think going to watch a film gives us so many significant and poignant memories. I think for me personally, I can't smell popcorn without putting myself in the foyer of a cinema. Are there any particular sweets or refreshments that you can remember going to the seat with?

P.E. I was also thinking about that because my mum was quite strict about us having sweets and popcorn and anything like that. I expect we were allowed to take a bottle of water and have a sip because that was how life was – we weren't really allowed sweets. It's funny because I went on and ended up working in an independent cinema. I used to be the Programming and Education Assistant at the Watershed [Cinema] in Bristol. In an art-house cinema, you don't really eat in the cinema. It's when you go to your multiplexes that you get your big bags of popcorn.

So I've kind of got this sort of duel thing, depending on what the film is; you go in and you either go into the dark and you concentrate, or you go and have a massive box of popcorn – and get sticky feet. And they are very different but really lovely experiences, and there's room for both. I love going to the cinema.

I am sad that the Palace closed because I love going to the cinema. I wish that it had been developed and made better earlier on because it would have made more people go there rather than choosing to go to other venues. It became quiet – and this is because of my background – it was harder going when the sound wasn't as good and the pitch wasn't as sharp; when you've worked in a cinema and you know how it can be. And I think the best way to see a film is when it is given the best platform to see it.

When you see a film on a big screen with loads of people, it's just... it can be life-changing.

C.S. Many thanks Pip for taking the time to share your memories about the Palace Cinema.

> 'WHEN YOU SEE A FILM ON A BIG SCREEN WITH LOADS OF PEOPLE...IT CAN BE LIFE-CHANGING.'

DO YOU HAVE ANY FURTHER COMMENTS?

YES, THIS MAKES ME SO ANGRY. IT SHOULD NOT BE ALLOWED. ALTON DOESN'T NEED ANY MORE NEW HOUSING. THIS BUILDING WAS BEAUTIFUL ONCE AND COULD BE AGAIN! [...] IT'S A MASSIVE SHAME.

I wish there was a way for the cinema to be restored so that we can keep it forever.

If you go to a cinema and feel welcome and engaged by the programming and people involved, there is a lovely enhancement to the emotion of sharing the films themselves.

WE LOVE THE PALACE.

I don't want it to go. I'm a teen who cant drive to Basingstoke and I don't want to take a bus at 7pm so walking to my local cinema is so great. I've grown up with this cinema and in my opinion is one of the more interesting things to do in Alton.

A cinema in Alton is viable. Hopefully it will have one again at some point. It does not need to be at the current location.

My father came to watch *Mamma Mia 2* with me in 2018 a few weeks before he died, it has very emotional ties for me now as it was my last ever Daddy date.

WISH WE COULD KEEP IT OPEN SOMEHOW.

This building is a historic part of Alton and a place where friends can meet up to watch a movie together. it is better for the environment because you don't need to drive out of town. It encourages people to stay local... my friends and I have been down to the local pub after watching a film together, or have gone for food afterwards. I think it's very short sighted letting this cinema close.

I will certainly miss the cinema here, it's a local landmark and it would be nice if it were purchased an refurbished.

I HOPE WE WILL FIND ANOTHER WAY TO VIEW FILMS IN A CINEMA ENVIRONMENT IN ALTON.

HOW DID YOU HEAR ABOUT THE MEMORIES OF THE PALACE CINEMA ORAL HISTORY PROJECT?

WORD OF MOUTH

FLYER

Abbe Fletcher is my mother

NEWSPAPERS

INVITATION

Alton
Herald

EMAIL
LIST

SOCIAL
MEDIA

Emailed Memories

FROM: Chris Holden

SUBJECT: My friends and I miss the Palace

I went to see a film about two disabled young men who wanted to live in the community rather than a home. It was called (if I remember correctly) *In My Head I'm Dancing*. The film started and within five minutes it flickered and stopped. I sat there for a couple of minutes wondering what was going to happen next. The doors were flung open, several students came in from Treloars, were settled into a space and then the film started up again. How wonderful to have that caring service so the students didn't miss anything.

My second memory is my husband and I settled in to watch a film. There was a tap on my husband's shoulder to say come and speak to your daughter on the lobby phone. There had been a family emergency but she knew we would have turned our phones off and were not contactable for a couple of hours. One of the staff had ticked our names off the list and knew where we were sitting. Again, what wonderful service.

My friends and I miss the Palace and always chose coming to our Alton cinema rather than go to Basingstoke.

Chris Holden

I moved to Alton about thirty-one years ago for a new job having previously lived in Norwich. I didn't know anyone, apart from new work colleagues and a family I lodged with initially. There was a film showing at The Palace which I had tried to see in Norwich before leaving but it was so popular I had not been able to, I think it was *Presumed Innocent* with Harrison Ford. It was showing at the Palace so I went along I think on a Sunday to a 5 pm performance. While buying a ticket I had a conversation with the chap in the ticket office who also came from Norwich. As he was also acting as the usher he then took me into the cinema which was completely empty and asked where I would like to sit. I was so amazed at an empty cinema I asked whether the film would actually be shown! He assured me it would even if no one else came and then told me that as it was a long film they usually had a ten minute interval for ice cream etc. and did I want an interval? I didn't so he said we wouldn't have one as he was also the projectionist. He then added that he usually had a cup of coffee half way through the film and would I like one.

So that was my first experience of the Palace, sitting in the middle of the back row with a cup of coffee half way through with only the projectionist and another usherette/ice cream seller for an audience. I have been many times since then but never had the luxury of my own private cinema! Although I am unable to go to the cinema through decreasing mobility I shall be very sorry if the Palace were to no longer operating in Alton. As a life-long cinema goer, films have been a hugely important part of my life, I would like to think, if it could be saved and renovated, it would provide future generations of cinema goers with the enjoyment and culture that the wonderful world of films provide.

Helen Brewin

FROM: Alton Lions Club

SUBJECT: Alton Lions Club has fond memories of the Palace Cinema

Alton Lions Club has fond memories of the Palace Cinema.

Thanks to the benevolence of Raj Jeyasingam, over the latter years the Club was able to hold a series of charity film nights at the Palace which provided a great deal of fun and raised many hundreds of pounds for local charities.

A favourite was *The Best Exotic Marigold Hotel* which saw visitors ascending the staircase beneath an arch of marigolds to be greeted with drinks and canapés before taking their seats for an evening of laughter. The blockbuster had only recently been released and yet here it was, in full glory, at the Palace!

Moira Baker, President of the Alton Lions Club

FROM: Françoise Galley

SUBJECT: A small contribution

1982 - *Bambi* was shown so I decided to take my two daughters to the cinema. As they were 2 and 4 or thereabout, we sat at the end of a row by the door, just in case and right at the back so the girls could sit on top of the chair back, resting against the wall. They were very excited but the excitement turned into tears when Bambi's mummy was killed. My youngest daughter was so upset that I had to take her out of the auditorium, explaining to the older one that I would be just round the corner outside. The toddler eventually calmed down and we returned but I cannot say this first cinema experience was a full success and I certainly would not take my grandchildren to see the film!

Françoise

FROM: Paul Cartwright

SUBJECT: Great fun

Hi Abbe,

Hope you don't mind the random email, but was telling my daughter about when I used to be a film projectionist. This led me to googling the cinema I worked, which led me to you and your research.

So my relationship with the cinema was varied to say the least. Firstly, I used to lodge with the wife of one of the owners at a time when the cinema used to hold wrestling shows.

My next interaction was when I helped run a mobile disco – we used to put a disco on for the kids in the town on a Wednesday evening.

I then ended up working in the cinema as a projectionist (when they were showing films three or four nights a week) and in the bingo hall – a mixed role indeed.

I saw that you were possible writing a book? Would love to get a copy once it has finished. Also, what happened to everything that was in the cinema? I guess it would have changed a lot since my time – back then it was the traditional film canisters! Wednesday afternoon would be prepping the adverts for the weekend shows. Great fun.

Anyway, I think I'm a bit late to the party for the work you have been doing, but I thought I would reach out.

Kind regards,
Paul

Hi Abbe,

Good to hear from you. I only have one photo from that period, with *Neighbours* superstar Geoff Paine who played Dr Clive Gibbons, from 1988.

Back in those days you used to have a national bingo game which took place in the middle of the evening. What this meant was all the money taken across participating bingo halls was put in one pot thus generating quite a decent prize fund
As the bingo caller, you knew if you had a big winner and on one evening I was calling when I realised one of our ladies would be getting the big prize which I think would have been around £30,000.

Anyway, Geoff was our special guest to present the prize. Funniest thing was that by then he was no longer in *Neighbours* as the show was about two years behind Australia!

With regards the cinema side, we used to have two old projectors that used carbon rods to produce the light. On a Wednesday the film canisters would arrive and you would make the film up – add a leader and tail, plus create your advertising film.

You had to be careful with the projectors as occasionally the film could get caught in the 'gate' and would then catch fire creating a flare on the screen!

Worst mistake I ever made was mixing up the reels. Generally films are five reels long and they would sit under a work bench in order. One evening I managed to mix them up playing reel one, followed by reel three, then reel two! It was only half way through this reel I realised my error but it was too late to do anything about it. I remember going down to the foyer afterwards and hearing some very confused customers talking about the movie they had just watched.

The projection box was situated behind the facade of the cinema. On a summers evening you could stand outside with a lovely view of the town. Fond memories.

I haven't been back to the cinema since the 80s, and only occasionally return to Alton when visiting family who live in Lasham. Sad to hear it is closing, love these old buildings. Loved my time working there!

Regards

Paul

Paul Cartwright with Geoff Paine (who played Dr Clive Gibbons in Neighbours) on stage to award prizes at the Palace Cinema in 1988, before the cinema was divided into two screens.
Photo © Paul Cartwright

MEMORIES
OF THE
PALACE
CINEMA

ORAL HISTORY PROJECT

THE PALACE IS CLOSED
..BUT THE MEMORIES LIVE ON

19th November 2022 2-4pm
Alton Community Centre

Come and share your memories
of the Palace and of cinema-going
in Alton for our Oral History Project

ALL WELCOME

Just turn up and have a chat with us.

memoriesofthepalace@gmail.com
@memoriesofthepalacecinemaalton

Memories of the Palace Cinema Oral History Project flyer, 2022.
Photo © Abbe Fletcher

GUILD OF OPTIMISTS

Afterword
Cinema in Alton

At the end of this project, what resonates is the fondness that people have for the Palace Cinema and that their memories of going there form a part of their lives. There is an attitude that with streaming platforms, people can just watch films at home, but this denies us the opportunity to commune with others and leaves us in our homes, having isolated, disconnected experiences of those films.

On Sunday, 30th October 2022, I woke up thinking of the cinema and that I must go that day to talk to Raj. When I arrived, he told me that this was the final day and the Palace would be closed starting tomorrow. Raj very kindly showed me around, giving me the whole tour behind the scenes. I am very grateful to him for this. On my way out, I met the newly appointed community and outreach officer for the Allen Gallery, Nancy Peskett, who was bringing her son to the cinema one last time. This serendipitous meeting prompted a collaboration between Memories of the Palace Cinema and the Allen Gallery to start a community pop-up cinema at the Gallery. We applied for and were awarded a grant and training from Cinema For All and the BFI and in March 2023, we started our programme with a screening of Aftersun and then a screening of *Sherlock Junior* for the Friendship Café. We have been screening films monthly at the Screen at the Allen Gallery. To date, we have shown *Woman at War, Brief Encounter, Love and Friendship, Barbie, It's a Wonderful Life* and *Lunana: A Yak in the Classroom*. Each screening has been sold out and the audience has had a hushed reverence and appreciation for watching a film on a big(ish) screen together.

Cinema came to Alton early last century and the Palace has been an essential part of our town's history for 110 years, and as an early purpose-built cinema, part of the country's rich cinema history. It underwent many alterations and modernisations to adapt to the changing technology and audiences. We hope that we can continue to screen films in Alton including going back to where they were first screened in 1902 at the Assembly Rooms, and branching out into other venues around the town, to adapt and provide communal cinema experiences long into the future.

Acknowledgements

There are so many people to thank for their help with this project. Firstly thank you to Raj Jeyasingam for keeping the Palace Cinema open for 28 years. Generations have grown up going to the Palace thanks to you.

Thank you to the Save Alton Cinema group. Thank you to Kat Guenioui and Annie Lancaster – fellow Optimists for giving that initial boost – that this could be a project and supporting it – all the way.

Thank you Helen Dudley for your encouragement and help with applying to the Alton Society. Thank you Tim Woolman for your support and encouragement and for organising interviews and putting on screenings.

Thank you Carol Planner for your encouragement and editing skills. Thank you Rebecca Slama for designing our flyers. Thank you Riana Gallager for kind words on my spiel early on.

Special thanks to Chris Stone from Wey Valley Radio who promoted our project from the start and came to our launch in September 2022 and who has contributed his fantastic interview skills.

Thank you to the Alton Society for awarding the project a grant to get started.

Thank you to the Guild of Optimists for administering the grant.

Very special thanks to local historian Jane Hurst whose research and knowledge on the history of Alton is encyclopaedic – thank you for taking the time to inspire and indulge me and for sourcing information and spreading the word about the project.

Heartfelt thanks to everyone who filled out a questionnaire and shared their memories of going to the Palace Cinema.

Thank you to everyone we interviewed, particularly those who agreed we could include their interviews in this book: Alison White, Simon Wood, Ellora Sutton, Pip Eldridge, Tim Woolman, Joan Andrews, Geraldine Dawson, Robert Booker, Jo Holmes and Mandy O'Neill. Thank you for taking the time to talk with us and record your memories and observations about the Palace, and about cinema-going in general. Thank you again Raj Jeyasingam, for your contribution to the book and for the photo of the Full House sign.

Thank you to the Curtis Museum volunteers who spread the word about the project, and the many who filled out questionnaires themselves.

Thank you to Nancy Peskett at the Allen Gallery for all the work that has gone into our pop-up cinema there. Thank you to the volunteers at the Allen Gallery and everyone who has come to a screening there. Thank you to Cinema for All, for supporting the Screen at the Allen Gallery with a grant and training to get us started in January 2023.

Thank you to Amery Hill School who allowed us to have a stand at their winter fayre in 2022 and to the students who filled out questionnaires.

Thank you to all questionnaire respondents: Catherine Buckland, Julie Alexander, David Finden, Gordon Smyth, R Madleen, Shelley, Jo Holmes, Paul Luis, Maisey Bell, Fran Clements, Jean Cornelius, M Knight, Drew Calver, Annette Bushnell, Tony, Sonia Clark, Lois Leonard, Donna Wood, Rob Lane, Helen Dudley, Keren Burney, Kathy Robertson, Ruth Hazeldine, Kate Bentley, John Bentley, Eleanor Hill, Laeton, Thomas Evans, Imogen Wood, Tye, Isabelle, Rosie Lane, Mary and many anonymous contributors.

Special thanks to Ginny Boxall, Corinna Downing, Mick Collins, Catharine Des Forges and Phil Clapp for your support of the project and your kind and inspiring words.

Thank you to Alton Library, where our Record Your Memories flyers were seen and people got in touch or filled out questionnaire as a result. Thank you to Tony Cross and Phillip Bagg for photographs of the Palace Cinema over the years.

Thank you to Tim Waters for securing and sharing the incredible 1913 photograph of the Alton Picture Theatre in the eleventh hour.

Thank you to Mick Collins who has been most generous in his support and encouragement. His fantastic book on The Cinemas of R. A Thomas (2015) is a testament to the impact that memories of a beloved Cinema can produce such a valuable resource.

Thank you to Stephen Dick at Holybourne Rare Books for the Belles of St. Trinian's Palace Cinema advertisement poster and thank you to Raj for permission to include the poster in the book.

Thank you to all at Goldfinch Books.

Thank you to Aram Atkinson, Nelson Douglas, Shane O'Sullivan, Emma Tait and Simon Brown at Kingston School of Art for their encouragement.

Extra special thanks to Ally McAlpine, Veronica S. Rodriguez, Gemma Haines and Sam Mangan, from the MA Publishing Course at Kingston University for taking up this project and designing such a beautiful book for us and for your patience and attention to detail.

On a personal note, thank you to my family for putting up with my cinema memories obsession over the past few years. Thank you Lois Leonard, my daughter and co-researcher from the start, whose enthusiasm, humour and imagination kept me going through this project. Thank you to Frank W. Leonard for his patience with all things cinema-related. Thank you to Dan for enduring and supporting my cinema geekdom .

Thank you to my Mum, Shielagh for her tireless encouragement and love. Thank you to Richard Fletcher, Rebeka Campos Astorkiza and my nephew Eneko Campos Fletcher for their encouragement from afar.

Thank you to everyone who stopped and talked to us and shared their memories of cinema-going in Alton. As Ellora Sutton says in her interview: a cinema is more than just a cinema, it is the people in it and it can tell a story of a town.

Alton needs a cinema.

We weren't able to save the cinema, but we succeeded in igniting a conversation and connecting people who shared the same interests. As a direct result of our campaign, we now have pop-up cinema in Alton and an Arts Festival in the works. None of this would be possible without the enthusiasm of our community.

Thank you, Abbe, for recording these memories and giving our town a voice. Your tireless efforts to preserve the legacy of the Palace Cinema and kickstart a new cinema experience in town will be appreciated by generations to come.

Guild of Optimists

Bibliography

Atwell, D. (1980) Cathedrals of the Movies: A History of British Cinemas and their Audiences, The Architectural Press: UK

Barker, J., Brown, R. & Gree r, W. (1981) The Cinemas of Portsmouth: A Nostagic `reminder of the Picture Palaces of Portsmouth, Gosport, Fareham and Cosham, Milestones Publications: UK

Collins, M. (2015) The Cinemas of R. A. Thomas, published by Mick Collins: UK

Eyles, A. (2005) Old Cinemas, Shire: UK

Giles, J (2018) The Scala Cinema 1978 – 1993, FAB Press: UK

Hawkins, C. W. (1973) The Story of Alton, published by Alton Urban Council: UK

Hurst, Jane (2011) 'Everything of the Best' The Early Days of Alton's Picture Palace' Alton Papers Number 15, 2011 pp34-39

Marchand, Y. & Meffre, R. (2021) Movie Theatres, Prestel Verlag, Munich London New York: Germany

Sharp, D. (1969) The Picture Palace: and other buildings for the movies, Hugh Evelyn London: UK

Stokes, M., Jones, M. & Pett , E., (Eds) (2022) Cinema Memories: A People's History of Cinema-Going in 1960s Britain, Bloomsbury: UK

Wickham, P. (2010) The Bill Douglas Cinema Museum Guide Book, University of Exeter: UK

Williams, D. R. (1993) Cinema in Leicester 1896-1931, Heart of Albion Press: UK

Williams, D. R, (2004) Cinema in a Cathedral City: Durham 1896-2003, Mercia Cinema Society: UK

Memories of Alton Oral History Project, Local Studies Collection at the Curtis Museum

Picture Mad: Andover's Cinemas Past and Present
https://www.andoverfilmclub.org/picture-mad/

Reel Stories: An Oral History of London's Projectionists
https://www.reelstories.org.uk/kingston/

The History of the Everyman Cinema Hampstead 1934 – 2000 by Margret O'Brien
https://everymancinemahistory.co.uk/

Scala!!! (2023) Dir. Jane Giles & Ali Catterall
https://www.bfi.org.uk/bfi-film-releases/scala

Bill Douglas Cinema Museum
https://www.bdcmuseum.org.uk/

Cinema For All
https://cinemaforall.org.uk/

Independent Cinema Office
https://www.independentcinemaoffice.org.uk/

UK Cinema Association
https://www.cinemauk.org.uk/

British Film Institute
https://www.bfi.org.uk/

Biographies

ABBE FLETCHER is an Alton resident and senior lecturer in the Department of Film & Photography at Kingston School of Art, Kingston University. She is course leader for the MA film making and a filmmaker and researcher. She is also a ceramics research volunteer at the Allen Gallery and Film Programmer for the Screen at the Allen Gallery pop-up Cinema there. She was inspired by hearing people share their memories of the Palace Cinema whilst campaigning to save the cinema in 2022 and set up the Memories of the Palace Cinema Alton Oral History Project to capture these memories and the love and appreciation for a cinema in Alton.

TIM WOOLMAN moved to Alton in 2007, looking to enjoy walking to the Palace Cinema alongside other local attractions. Working at the University for the Creative Arts, in 2012 he joined those interested to support the Alton Independent Cinema Project formed in response to the Palace Cinema being put up for sale. When it was no longer for sale, he invited those interested in the Project to see what was possible in terms of broadening the provision for film locally. With several others he formed Experience Film. They showed 30 films beginning with The Last Projectionist, partly a story of the Electric Cinema in Birmingham which coincidentally Tim used to go to. Experience Film continued until 2017 thanks to Chris Campbell and Pete Day, proving there was an interest in a wide range of film. Also, that local venues such as Wessex Arts at Alton College, could host films, including those chosen for Regency Week. It was a good experience showing 2001: A Space Odyssey at Winchester Planetarium and combining films with, for example, a jazz band or a magician. Silent films with live piano accompaniment at Frensham Heights School were a particular favourite.

When the Palace Cinema was put up for sale again in 2021, Tim joined the Save Alton Cinema group and collated responses to the survey about the cinema. He has been happy to help others record their memories of the Palace Cinema in Alton, following the marvellous lead of Abbe Fletcher, encouraged also by Chris Stone from Wey Valley Radio. With the chance to show films at the Allen Gallery since March 2023, people continue to talk about what could be good for Alton.

While offering no substitute for a historic cinema like the Palace, Tim continues to explore how to help those who would like to extend the local options for experiencing film.

KAT GUENIOUI is an Alton resident and a firm believer in the power of community and creativity. She set up the Guild of Optimists together with Annie Lancaster in December 2021 when they launched the campaign to save the Palace Cinema.

CHRIS STONE is an experienced Primary School Teacher with a history of working in the primary education industry. Presenter on Wey Valley radio 101.1 FM every Wednesday and Thursday afternoon 2 to 5 pm, including regular interviews with guests. He has lived in Alton since the late 1990s and was very lucky to get involved with Wey Valley Radio not long after settling here. It's given him the opportunity to speak to many interesting people in and around Alton. When he was asked if would record some interviews on capturing memories of the Palace, he was very happy to help.

CAROL PALMER a past Committee member of The Burton Civic Society, and now the Alton Society, and local campaigner.

JANE HURST Local historian, researcher, author of books and articles, leader of walks and giver of talks about local people and places.

THE GUILD OF OPTIMISTS was established in December 2021 with the launch of the 'Save the Cinema' campaign, which aimed to prevent the closure and demolition of the Palace Cinema. Though that campaign was unsuccessful, the Guild of Optimists went on to other projects, including town-wide litter picks, a litter pick lending library, planting a hedge along the road-facing front of a local infant school, and organising a climate action protest in Alton. The Guild of Optimists has since spawned a new endeavour - the Alton Arts Festival CIC, which will brings its inaugural 10-day multi-discipline festival to the town in July 2024.

THE ALTON SOCIETY is a local charity which was formed in 1970 at a public meeting as a reaction to the threat to Alton's historical identity by the proposal to demolish the former Inwood Cottage Hospital.

It celebrated its 50th anniversary at the Maltings recently. The Society is proud to be able to support the Memories of the Palace Cinema and other local projects and organisations through its Grant Scheme.

Amongst its aims are:
· To encourage appropriate development of Alton and its amenities, while also resisting undesirable changes.
· To stimulate interest in the town's past, present, and future.
· To preserve and enhance features of particular historical, cultural, aesthetic, and environmental importance.
· To provide a forum for public discussion.
· To advance the Society's views to the authorities concerned and to the wider community

https://altonsociety.wordpress.com/about/

thealtonsociety@gmail.com

Also by Abbe Fletcher

'Film maker in the family: the impact of family life on creativity'. Deepwell, Katy (ed.). *Feminist Activisms and Artivisms*. (2019)   Amsterdam, Netherlands: Valiz.

'2/60 48 Köpfe aus dem Szondi-Test'. Hamlyn, Nicky. Payne, Simon. Rees, A.L. (eds.). *Kurt Kren: Structural Films* (2016). [2/60 48 Heads from the Szondi-Test]. Bristol, U.K. : Intellect Books.

Selected Filmography

Future Ruins Future Archives (short film about the Ben Kelly Design Archive) [Producer] 2024

Hans Coper Spade Vase, 2023 short film made as ceramics research volunteer at the Allen Gallery, Alton [Director] 2023

About Making: Exploring Building Craft and its Social Processes [Co-Director/Videographer for UK-based episodes] 2021-22, funded by the British Council

Railwaywomen (short film shot on the Mid Hants Railway, Alresford, Ropely & Alton) [Director] 2018

The road to Gibara/El Camino Hacia Gibara (short film about the Cine Pobre No Budget Film Festival in Southern Cuba) [Co-Director] 2010

Four shores: artworks for the Isle of Sheppey Leigh-Fletcher, Abbe [Creator/Director], Turner, Stephen [Contributor], Barber, Ros [Contributor] and Barker, Simon [Contributor] (Documentary commissioned by the Arts Council and Kent County Council) 2005

About Kingston University Press

Kingston University Press has been publishing high-quality commercial and academic titles for over ten years. Our list has always reflected the diverse nature of the student and academic bodies at the university in ways that are designed to impact on debate, to hear new voices, to generate mutual understanding and to complement the values to which the university is committed.

Increasingly the books we publish are produced by students on the MA Publishing and BA Publishing courses, often working with partner organisations to bring projects to life. While keeping true to our original mission, and maintaining our wide-ranging backlist titles, our most recent publishing focuses on bringing to the fore voices that reflect and appeal to our community at the university as well as the wider reading community of readers and writers in the UK and beyond.

@KU_press

This book was edited, designed, typeset and produced by students on the MA Publishing course at Kingston University, London.

To find out more about our hands-on, professionally focused and flexible MA and BA programmes please visit:

www.kingston.ac.uk
www.kingstonpublishing.wordpress.com
@kingstonjourno

www.ingramcontent.com/pod-product-compliance
Lightning Source LLC
LaVergne TN
LVHW010316070426
835513LV00021B/2403